DC for Free

D C

FOR FREE

REVISED EDITION

HUNDREDS
OF FREE THINGS
TO DO
IN WASHINGTON, DC

BRIAN BUTLER

Mustang Publishing
Memphis, TN

Once again—
for Bonnie,
who makes it all happen.

Distributed to the trade by National Book Network, Lanham, MD.

8-30·94 9.00

Library of Congress Cataloging-in-Publication Data:
Butler, Brian, 1950-
    DC for free / Brian Butler. -- Rev. ed.
        p.   cm.
    ISBN 0-914457-62-4 (pbk.)
    1. Washington (D.C.) -- Guidebooks.   2. Washington
Region -- Guidebooks.   I. Title.
F192.3.B88   1994
917.5304'4 -- dc20   93-21119
                                                                            CIP

16832818

Printed on acid-free paper.
10 9 8 7 6 5 4 3 2 1

Contents

Acknowledgments

A wealth of people and organizations provided the information that made this book a reality. I would like to express my sincere gratitude to the following: Gary Dlacich of the Washington DC Convention and Visitors Association, Dave Halperin of the Metropolitan Area Transit Authority, the Alexandria Tourist Council, Ray Hogle of the Arlington Visitors Service, the Virginia Division of Tourism, the Montgomery County Travel Council, Prince William County Tourism Services, Prince Georges County Travel Council, Fairfax County Tourism Bureau, the National Park Service, the folks from the Visitor Information Center at 1455 Pennsylvania Avenue, and Geralynn Karpiscak.

Brian Butler

Introduction

Washington, DC is renowned for its marble monuments, great museums, and celebrated sights, but few of the 18 million annual visitors to America's capital know that hundreds of the best attractions and events are absolutely **free.**

DC for Free will help visitors and residents alike discover national shrines, priceless works of art, world-class museums, palatial mansions, ancient documents, the inner-workings of government, treasures of American heritage, gracious gardens, colorful festivals, exciting zoos, concerts, galleries, historical pageants, moving ceremonies, showcases of science and technology, behind-the-scenes-tours, and much more. And it's all free!

This guidebook is organized geographically by neighborhood, district, town, suburb, and map quadrant: the Mall, Capitol Hill, the White House and Foggy Bottom, Downtown, Northwest, Northeast, Southwest, Southeast, Georgetown, Arlington, Alexandria, suburban Virginia, and suburban Maryland. Each entry provides pertinent background information, admission days and hours, address, and phone number. Key codes indicate attractions within walking distance of Metrorail stations, sites with hassle-free access for people with limited mobility, entries that children will find enjoyable and entertaining, and attractions that offer free tours.

A simple caveat before you begin: time changes everything, including hours, phone numbers, and admission policies.

Every effort has been made to assure accuracy at the time of publication, but bear in mind that changes will occur, and some attractions that were free at press time may charge a fee now.

We welcome your comments or suggestions for future editions of *DC for Free*. Please write to me in care of Mustang Publishing, P.O. Box 3004, Memphis, TN 38173.

KEY	
M	**Metrorail nearby**
H	**Handicapped accessible**
C	**Appealing to children**
T	**Tours offered**

Getting Around

When visiting DC, it's best to have a mental map of the city in mind and a good street map in hand. Once you understand the city's grid system, it's remarkably easy to get around.

With the Capitol building serving as the grid's center, DC is divided into four quadrants: Northwest, Northeast, Southeast, and Southwest. Therefore, every city address is followed by the appropriate initials—NW, NE, SE, or SW. The demarcation lines are North Capitol Street, South Capitol Street, East Capitol Street, and the Mall.

Streets running north and south are numbered up to the 50's; those running east and west are lettered in alphabetical order (but there's no J, X, Y, or Z Street). Where the first alphabet ends, two-syllable names begin—Adams, Barry, Chaplin, etc. The grid is also crisscrossed by diagonal avenues named for states.

Street numbers are helpful in pinpointing DC addresses. For example, the White House, 1600 Pennsylvania Ave. NW, is located at 16th Street and Pennsylvania Avenue. For lettered streets, count one block per alphabet letter. Hence, K Street is ten blocks from A Street.

The best way to get around DC is by Metro, which has four lines in operation and a fifth under construction. Radiating from downtown DC, Metrorail offers a quick and easy way to get around town. Reaching deep into the Virginia and Mary-

Metrorail System Map

land suburbs, this 100-mile system operates weekdays, 5:30am to midnight; Saturdays, 8:00am to midnight; and Sundays, 10:00am to midnight.

Metro stations are marked by tall brown pylons topped with the letter M and colored bands that designate the Metro lines serving that stop.

The Metro uses a cashless fare system called "Farecard." You must purchase a card from vending machines located at each stop. The value of the card is encoded on a magnetic strip. To make travel more convenient, buy sufficient fare for a roundtrip. A great way to save money on weekends is the "Family Tourist Pass." For just $6, any group of four can travel on the Metro all day on any Saturday, Sunday, or holiday.

A good way to get acquainted and oriented is to make the Washington Visitors Information Service at 1455 Pennsylvania Avenue NW, your first stop. The friendly staff will provide free maps, sightseeing brochures, weekly events calendars, and other valuable information. They are open 9:00am to 5:00pm Monday through Saturday (phone 202-789-7000).

The Mall

Washington Monument

Fashioned after the obelisks of ancient Egypt, this memorial to America's Founding Father soars 555 feet above the Capital skyline. An elevator whisks visitors to the top for magnificent views of DC, Virginia, and Maryland. The white marble monument took nearly 50 years to complete, with construction halted by fundraising problems, political squabbles, and the Civil War. *Hours:* April 1st to Labor Day: open daily, 8:00am-midnight; Labor Day to March 31st: open daily, 9:00am-5:00pm. *Address:* Constitution Ave. at 15th St., NW (202-426-6841). **M H C**

National Air and Space Museum

The world's most visited museum offers 23 impressive galleries showcasing the history of aviation from Kitty Hawk to the Skylab space station. The museum's collection includes the original Wright Brothers Flyer, Lindbergh's *Spirit of St. Louis,* John Glenn's Mercury space capsule, Gemini 4, Apollo 11, and an authentic space station, plus a dazzling array of rockets, jet fighters, hot-air balloons, and moon rocks. Other popular attractions are the state-of-the-art Einstein Planetarium, the Langley Theater, with its giant 5-story by 7-story screen, and a hands-on astronomical observatory. *Hours:* daily, 10:00am-5:30pm (Memorial Day-Labor Day: 10:00am-9:00pm). *Address:* 6th St. & Independence Ave., SW (202-357-1400). **M H C T**

Smithsonian Institution Building

Known affectionately as "The Castle," this turreted, red sandstone edifice is the oldest of the Smithsonian's museums. Designed by James Renwick Jr. and completed in 1855, it orig-

The Washington Monument

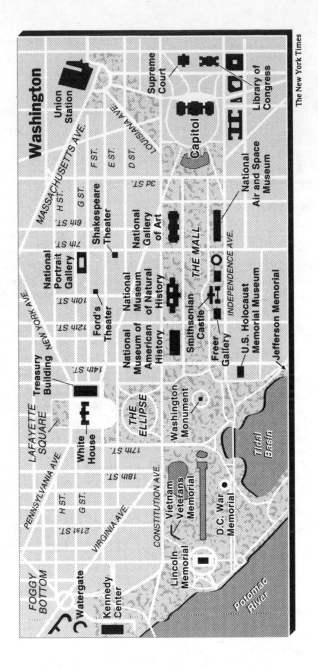

Washington

Union Station

MASSACHUSETTS AVE.

LOUISIANA AVE.

Supreme Court

Library of Congress

Capitol

The New York Times

H ST.

G ST.

F ST.

E ST.

D ST.

3d ST.

National Air and Space Museum

Shakespeare Theater

National Gallery of Art

7th ST.

THE MALL

National Portrait Gallery

9th ST.

10th ST.

INDEPENDENCE AVE.

National Museum of Natural History

Ford's Theater

12th ST.

Smithsonian Castle

U.S. Holocaust Memorial Museum

Jefferson Memorial

National Museum of American History

Freer Gallery

14th ST.

Treasury Building

LAFAYETTE SQUARE

PENNSYLVANIA AVE.

White House

THE ELLIPSE

Washington Monument

Tidal Basin

17th ST.

18th ST.

H ST.

G ST.

21st ST.

VIRGINIA AVE.

CONSTITUTION AVE.

Vietnam Veterans Memorial

D.C. War Memorial

FOGGY BOTTOM

Watergate

Kennedy Center

Lincoln Memorial

Potomac River

14

inally housed a science museum, art gallery, research labs, and the living quarters for the Smithsonian's Secretary and his family. Today, the Castle houses the Visitor Information & Reception Center, the Woodrow Wilson Center, administrative offices, and the tomb of James Smithson, founder of the Smithsonian Institution. *Hours:* daily, 10:00am-5:30pm. *Address:* 1000 Jefferson Dr., SW (202-357-1300). **M H T**

National Museum of Natural History
You'll have a difficult time deciding where to begin your tour of this spectacular museum. With more than 118 million items in its collections, the museum explores humanity's earliest history, the development of world cultures, plant and animal life, minerals and gems, the splendor of nature, and the dynamics of evolution. Highlights include a living coral reef, dinosaurs, Ice Age mammals, the Hope Diamond, the Insect Zoo, and the ever-popular Discovery Room, which offers children a hands-on approach to scientific research. *Hours:* daily, 10:00am-5:30pm (Memorial Day-Labor Day: 10:00am-7:30pm). *Address:* 10th St. & Constitution Ave., NW (202-357-2700 or 357-2747). **M H C T**

National Museum of American History
The diversity and magnitude of this Smithsonian museum's collection has earned the Institution its nickname "The Nation's Attic." Virtually several museums under one roof, with over 16 million objects in its collections, the Museum of American History embodies the nation's cultural, political, scientific, and technological heritage. Visitors will find exhibits on transportation, military history, agriculture, medicine, Colonial life, immigration, fashion, popular culture, communication, and much, much more. It's all here—from George Washington's false teeth to Nancy Reagan's inaugural gown. *Hours:* daily 10:00am-5:30pm (summer: 10:00am-7:30pm). *Address:* 14th St. & Constitution Ave., NW (202-357-1481 or 357-2700). **M H C T**

Hirshhorn Museum & Sculpture Garden
This striking cylindrical gallery and the adjoining sculpture garden provide a home for the priceless modern art collection donated by Joseph Hirshhorn to the Smithsonian. Focusing on late 19th- and 20th-century painting and sculpture, the collection incorporates representative works by innovative artists

such as Rodin, Matisse, Calder, Degas, Picasso, Moore, Rothko, Nevelson, Pollack, Giacometti, Rivers, Hockney, and Warhol. *Hours:* daily, 10:00am-5:30pm (summer: 10:00am-7:30pm). *Address:* 7th St. & Independence Ave., SW (202-357-3235 or 357-2700). **M H T**

Holocaust Memorial Museum

Chartered by a unanimous act of Congress, this new national museum and memorial is dedicated to the task of educating Americans about one of the darkest chapters in human history. The Museum's permanent exhibition explores all aspects of the Holocaust. The Hall of Remembrance, a hexagonal, skylit memorial, is designed for reflection and contemplation. The Children's Wall, which incorporates 6,000 colorful tiles painted by U.S. school children, is dedicated to the 1.5 million children murdered by the Nazis. In the Hall of Knowledge, an interactive, computer-based learning center, visitors can access the Museum's vast collection of films, photos, oral histories, and recordings. Upon entering the Memorial, every visitor receives an "Identity Card" with the name and history of a Holocaust victim. Throughout the exhibit, you can update the card at computer terminals, and at the end you learn the victim's fate. *Hours:* daily, 10:00am-5:00pm. *Address:* 14th St. and Raoul Wallenberg Pl., SW (202-488-0400). **M H C T**

Vietnam Veterans Memorial

This understated but powerfully moving memorial to U.S. Vietnam veterans has become one of DC's most visited sites. Inscribed on the 500-foot black granite wall are the names of over 58,000 American military personnel who died in Vietnam. Few visitors fail to be touched by the polished panels and small tokens of remembrance left by comrades, friends, and loved ones. *Hours:* open 24 hours. *Address:* Constitution Ave. between Henry Bacon Dr. & 21st St., NW (202-426-6700). **H**

Abraham Lincoln Memorial

Designed in the style of a classical Greek temple, this splendid shrine to the "Great Emancipator" is one of the most beautiful sights in DC. Thirty-six white marble columns, symbolizing the 36 states of the Union at the time of Lincoln's death, enshrine Daniel Chester French's somber statue of the President. Words from Lincoln's two greatest speeches—the Second Inaugural

The Lincoln Memorial

Address and the Gettysburg Address—are carved on the interior walls. *Hours:* open 24 hours. *Address:* Memorial Circle & 23rd St., SW (202-426-6841). **H C T**

National Gallery of Art
The National Gallery of Art presents one of the world's finest collections of American and European art from the 13th century to the present. The museum encompasses two radically different gallery buildings: the neoclassical West Building (one of America's largest marble structures) and the dramatically angular East Building, made of two interlocking triangles. Treasures to be discovered in the West Building's maze of galleries include works by Raphael, da Vinci, Botticelli, El Greco, Rembrandt, Vermeer, Monet, Renoir, Constable, and Peale. The East Building features works by such luminaries as Calder, Moore, Picasso, Mondrian, Matisse, Dali, and Miro. *Hours:* Mon-Sat, 10:00am-5:00pm; Sun, noon-9:00pm. *Address:* 4th St. & Constitution Ave., NW (202-737-4215). **M H T**

Arts and Industries Building
Capture the spirit of the 19th century with a visit to the Smithsonian's Arts and Industries showcase. This brick and sandstone extravaganza was erected in 1881 to house memorabilia from the 1876 Centennial Exhibition held in Philadelphia. Today, its four halls and rotunda recall the ambiance of the Victorian era with displays of home furnishings, costumes, industrial technology, militaria, and exhibits from the 37 states that comprised the Union at the time of the Centennial. *Hours:* daily, 10:00am-5:30pm (summer: 10:00am-7:30pm). *Address:* 900 Jefferson Dr., SW (202-357-2700 or 357-1500). **M H C T**

Museum of African Art
In 1987, the Smithsonian opened this unique museum dedicated to the collection, study, and exhibition of the arts and cultures of sub-Saharan Africa. The intriguing displays of works in wood, fiber, ivory, clay, metal, and stone are housed in an equally engaging underground gallery behind the Castle. Permanent exhibits are supplemented by special traveling shows from international collections. *Hours:* daily, 10:00am-5:30pm (summer: 10:00am-7:30pm). *Address:* 950 Independence Ave., SW (202-357-4600). **M H T**

The Jefferson Memorial

Thomas Jefferson Memorial

With its white marble colonnade and soaring neoclassical rotunda, the Jefferson Memorial reflects our third President's preference for the architecture of ancient Rome. Inside, there's a dignified bronze of Jefferson by Rudolph Evans and marble panels inscribed with quotes from the Declaration of Independence. Park Service rangers give interpretive talks every half hour from 8:00am to midnight. *Hours:* open 24 hours. *Address:* South Basin Dr., SW (202-426-6822). **H C T**

International Gallery

Located in the Smithsonian's subterranean compound, the International Gallery presents exhibitions that focus on world cultures through films, festivals, concerts, dance, and multimedia shows. A popular early event was the Caribbean Festival, with a colorfully re-created island street complete with shops, restaurants, craftspeople, and tropical foliage. *Hours:* daily, 10:00am-5:30pm (summer hours determined yearly). *Address:* 1100 Jefferson Dr., SW (202-357-2700). **M H C**

Freer Gallery of Art

The elegant Florentine Renaissance facade of the Freer reflects the distinguished collection of art inside. Often overshadowed

Constitution Gardens (Photo: Bill Clark/National Park Service)

by the other Smithsonian museums, the Freer contains one of the foremost collections of Asian art in the West. Indian miniatures, Tibetan sculpture, Egyptian glassware, Byzantine icons, ancient Chinese porcelains, and Japanese jades are just a fraction of the exotica on display. If time is limited, be sure to see the fabulous Peacock Room. *Hours:* daily, 10:00am-5:30pm. *Address:* 12th St. & Jefferson Dr., SW (202-357-2104). **M H T**

Constitution Gardens
Government buildings once stood on the 50 acres of rolling, shaded land between the Washington Monument and the Lincoln Memorial. Today, this wooded park is a peaceful oasis from the tourist whirlwind. A memorial to the signers of the Declaration of Independence is situated on an island in the Garden's lake. *Hours:* open 24 hours. *Address:* Constitution Ave. & 18th St., NW. **H C**

Enid A. Haupt Garden
Weary DC visitors will find respite in this charming, four-acre garden atop the Smithsonian's underground museum complex. The park-like setting incorporates exquisite ornamental shrubbery, trees, and flowers, and features Victorian garden furniture, tea roses, and magnolias. *Hours:* daily, 7:00am to dusk. *Address:* 1000 Independence Ave., SW. **M H**

Sylvan Theatre
Big band concerts, Elizabethan dramas, puppet shows, and country music performances are just some of the free attractions offered at the outdoor Sylvan Theatre during warm weather months. Open May-September. *Address:* Washington Monument grounds (202-426-6700).

Arthur M. Sachler Gallery
Set behind the Castle and below the Haupt Garden, this exotic museum hosts changing exhibitions of Asian and Near Eastern art drawn from international collections and the permanent collection donated by the museum's namesake. Highlights include works in jade, precious metals, ceramics, wood, lacquerware, bronze, textiles, and rare, ancient manuscripts. *Hours:* daily, 10:00am-5:30pm. *Address:* 1050 Independence Ave., SW (202-357-2104). **M H T**

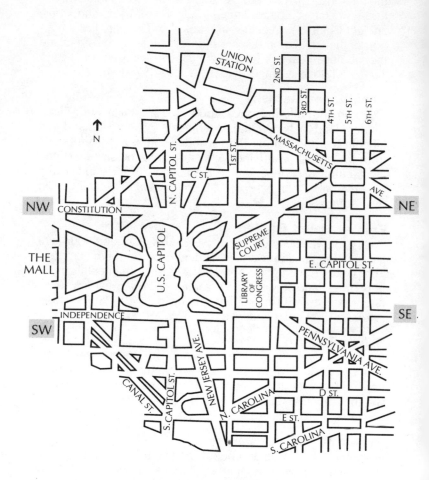

UNION STATION

2ND ST.
3RD ST.
4TH ST.
5TH ST.
6TH ST.

MASSACHUSETTS

N

N. CAPITOL ST.

1ST ST.

C ST.

AVE

NW   CONSTITUTION   NE

SUPREME COURT

THE MALL

U.S. CAPITOL

LIBRARY OF CONGRESS

E. CAPITOL ST.

INDEPENDENCE   SE

SW

NEW JERSEY AVE.

PENNSYLVANIA AVE.

CANAL ST.

S. CAPITOL ST.

N. CAROLINA

D ST.

E ST.

S. CAROLINA

Capitol Hill

Capitol Hill

Library of Congress

Without doubt the world's greatest documentary treasury, the Library of Congress houses a collection of 85 million items occupying 535 miles of shelves. Holdings include priceless manuscripts, films, recordings, rare books, maps, periodicals, photographs, prints, and documents. The spectacular building, lavishly decorated in a profusion of marbles, mosaics, murals, and stained glass, alone merits a visit. In addition to permanent exhibits, including the first drafts of the Declaration of Independence and the Gettysburg Address, a Gutenberg Bible, L'Enfant's original plan for Washington DC, and Mathew Brady's Civil War photographs, the Library hosts rotating shows, a weekly concert series, plays, and poetry recitals. Be sure to take the 40-minute guided tour, which begins with an interesting audio-visual show in the Orientation Theater. *Hours:* Mon-Fri, 8:30am-9:30pm; Sat, 8:30am-5:00pm; Sun, 1:00pm-5:00pm. (Tours run Mon-Fri, 9:00am-4:00pm.) *Address:* 1st St. & East Capitol St., SE (202-707-6400 or 707-5458). **M H T**

The Capitol

The magnificent white dome of the Capitol is DC's most enduring symbol of democratic government. Under the great cast-iron dome, Congress meets to shape law and policy. The best way to get to know the Capitol is to take the excellent tour. You'll see the majestic Rotunda, decorated with Brumidi's fres-

The U.S. Capitol

co glorifying George Washington, the 10-ton bronze Columbus Doors, which depict scenes from the life of the great explorer, Statuary Hall, the elegant old Supreme Court Chamber, the Crypt, the impressive House of Representatives, the dignified Senate Chamber, and much more. If possible, schedule your visit during Congressional working hours, when you'll be able to attend Senate and House sessions or Committee hearings. Write your Representative in advance requesting a Visitor's Pass, which will allow access to chamber balconies. Foreign visitors can obtain passes from the Doorkeeper of the House or Senate Sergeant-at-Arms. *Hours:* daily, 9:00am-4:30pm; Memorial Day through Labor Day: daily, 9:00am-8:00pm (tours: 9:00am to 3:45pm). *Address:* Capitol Hill (202-225-6827). **M H T**

U.S. Botanic Garden
Don't miss this refreshing oasis at the foot of Capitol Hill! After the weighty concerns of government, history, and culture, you can relax in this marvelous conservatory with its lush rainforest, palm trees, orchid display, streams, and gardens. Special seasonal exhibits include poinsettias, chrysanthemums, azal-

eas, lilies, tulips, primrose, and tropical plants. *Hours:* daily, 9:00am-5:00pm (June-August, 9:00am-9:00pm). *Address:* 1st St. & Maryland Ave., SW (202-225-8333). **M** **H** **C** **T**

Folger Shakespeare Library

The Folger Library is much more than the finest collection of Shakespeare memorabilia in the world; it's also an esteemed assemblage of Renaissance costumes, manuscripts, art works, books, and theatrical memorabilia. Inside the spare, neoclassical structure, there's an exuberant reproduction of an Elizabethan Great Hall. The barrel-vaulted gallery, with its oak paneling and tiled floor, has marvelous exhibits of musical instruments, European apparel, furniture, paintings, models, and a working Elizabethan theater used for plays, concerts, poetry readings, and lectures. *Hours:* Mon-Sat, 10:00am-4:00pm (tours Mon-Fri, 11:00am-1:00pm). *Address:* 201 East Capitol St., SE (202-5447077). **M** **C** **T**

Bartholdi Fountain

Frederic Auguste Bartholdi, sculptor of the Statue of Liberty, designed this flamboyant fountain as the centerpiece for the 1876 Centennial Exhibition in Philadelphia. It originally symbolized fire and water, with jets of flames and dancing cascades of water. After the Centennial, the fountain was transported to DC, and the gas jets were replaced by electric globes. The surrounding garden, with thousands of annual flowers, is spectacular in spring and autumn. *Address:* Independence Ave. between Canal & 1st St.

U.S. Grant Memorial

This is the largest sculptural grouping in DC and the second largest equestrian statue in the world. The immense bronze figure of President Ulysses S. Grant on his steed Cincinnatus depicts the Civil War hero as warrior rather than politician. The groupings at either end of the memorial represent a dramatic cavalry charge and a Civil War artillery unit in action. *Address:* 1st St. between Maryland & Pennsylvania Avenues.

The Supreme Court

Supreme Court

The nation's highest court is housed in a dazzling white marble building resembling an ancient Greek temple. The nine Justices hear cases in an august chamber with tall marble columns and a lofty, embellished ceiling. How you schedule your visit should depend on whether the Court is in session. The Supreme Court sits two weeks of every month, October to June. Visitor seating is limited and on a first-come, first-served basis, so come early. When the Court is not sitting, lectures are presented in the courtroom every half hour from 9:30am to 3:30pm, and tours of the building are possible. *Hours:* Mon-Fri, 9:00am-4:30pm. *Address:* 1st St. & Maryland Ave., NE (202-479-3030). **M H T**

Sewall-Belmont House

Alice Paul, author of the original Equal Rights Amendment and founder of the National Women's Party, lived and worked in the Sewall-Belmont House for many years. But women's suffrage was just one of the weighty issues debated there since the stately brick townhouse was built in 1799. During the early 19th century, both the Louisiana Purchase and the Treaty of Ghent were negotiated at this National Historic Site. Today, the mansion is filled with historic memorabilia and furnishings reflecting its ties to influential political figures from Daniel Webster to Susan B. Anthony. *Hours:* Tues-Fri, 10:00am-3:00pm; Sat-Sun, noon-4:00pm. *Address:* 144 Constitution Ave., NE (202-546-3989).

Taft Memorial

This memorial honors Senator Robert A. Taft of Ohio. A 27-bell carillon hangs in the marble tower set amidst a stand of red oak. At the base of the tower, there's a statue of "Mr. Republican," son of President William Howard Taft and three-time unsuccessful candidate for his party's presidential nomination. *Hours:* open 24 hours. (Carillon chimes at 1/4 hour intervals.) *Address:* Constitution Ave. between New Jersey & Louisiana Aves., NW.

Fountain of Neptune

Surrounding the Roman sea god Neptune is a fantastical array of sea nymphs and aquatic creatures. This delightful turn-of-the-century fountain, designed by Hinton Perry, is well worth a detour. *Hours:* open 24 hours. *Address:* 1st St. between East Capitol St. & Independence Ave.

The White House from the North Lawn

The White House Area

The White House

A visit to DC would be most incomplete without a tour of "The President's Palace." Each year, over 1.5 million tourists pass through the only official residence of a head of state that is open for public viewing on a regular basis. Unfortunately, you see only five of the mansion's 132 rooms on the whirlwind tour. However, you may be able to arrange a VIP guided tour that's more extensive. Write your Representative or Senator stating the date you wish to visit and the number of tickets you need. *Hours:* Tues-Sat, 10:00am-noon. (From late May through Labor Day, obtain tickets at the Ellipse booth beginning at 8:00am.) *Address:* 1600 Pennsylvania Ave., NW (202-456-7041 or 456-2000). **M H C T**

Renwick Gallery

Originally designed by James Renwick Jr. in 1859 to house financier William Corcoran's private art collection, this distinguished building now serves as a branch of the Smithsonian's National Museum of American Art. The Renwick provides a showcase for exhibits of contemporary design, textiles, porcelain, furniture, crafts, and decorative arts. Aside from its excellent shows, the Renwick merits a visit if only to enjoy the superbly restored Grand Salon. This opulent gallery, with its berry red walls and velvet banquettes, is one of the most beautiful halls in DC. *Hours:* daily, 10:00am-5:30pm. *Address:* Pennsylvania Ave. at 17th St., NW (202-357-2700). **M H T**

Organization of American States

This attractive building serves as the headquarters for the 32-nation Organization of American States. The interesting guided tour, in both English and Spanish, includes the Tropical Patio, Hall of Heroes, Hall of the Americas, Council Chamber, Aztec Garden, and art gallery. *Hours:* Mon-Fri, 9:00am-5:00pm (tours 9:30am-4:00pm). *Address:* 17th St. & Constitution Ave., NW (202-458-3751). **M T**

Museum of Modern Art of Latin America

Located adjacent to the OAS Aztec Garden, this unique museum is devoted entirely to the work of artists from the Caribbean and Central and Latin American. Rotating exhibits from the museum's permanent collection are displayed along with special exhibitions from international museums and private collections. Don't miss the vibrant self-taught art in the Folk Vision Gallery! *Hours:* Tues-Sat, 10:00am-5:00pm. *Address:* 201 18th St., NW (202-458-3000). **M T**

Daughters of the American Revolution Museum

The imposing Memorial Continental Hall houses the DAR's splendid collection of Americana. More than 40,000 objects, tracing the development of 17th, 18th, & 19th century America, are displayed in 33 period rooms and an immense gallery. Highlights of these rooms—maintained by state DAR chapters—include New Jersey's replica Colonial Council Chamber, Tennessee's room decorated with furnishings from James Monroe's White House, California's adobe homestead, and New York's elegant salon with 18th-century furnishings. *Hours:* Mon-Fri, 8:30am-4:00pm; Sun, 1:00pm-5:00pm. *Address:* 1776 D St., NW (202-879-3242). **M H C T**

Interior Department Museum

This museum describes the development of the Interior Department, the National Park Service, the Fish and Wildlife Service, the Geological Survey, and the Bureaus of Indian Affairs and Land Management. Dioramas depict historic events, such as the meeting of Washington and Lafayette and frontier life in the 19th century. Excellent displays of Native American crafts and artifacts make a visit worthwhile. *Hours:* Mon-Fri, 8:00am-4:00pm. *Address:* C St. between 18th & 19th Sts., NW (202-343-2743). **M H C T**

Corcoran Gallery of Art

With its ornate grillwork and copper roof, the Corcoran is one of DC's finest Beaux Arts buildings. Inside, the city's oldest art museum presents a marvelous collection including American landscapes, French Impressionists, Flemish masters, early photographs, medieval stained glass, Belgian tapestries, and the 18th-century Grand Salon from the Hotel D'Orsay in Paris, fully reconstructed, cherubs and all. In addition, the Corcoran stages monthly exhibitions, international shows, films, lectures, and a concert series. *Hours:* Tues-Sun, 10:00am-4:30pm (Thurs till 9:00pm). *Address:* 17th St. at New York Ave., NW (202-638-3211 or 638-1070). **M H T**

Department of State Diplomatic Reception Rooms

For a truly memorable experience, book a tour of the incomparable Diplomatic Reception Rooms. An entire floor of the State Department has been transformed into a showplace for 18th- and 19th-century decorative arts and furnishings. Highlights include the John Quincy Adams Drawing Room (used by the Secretary of State to receive official guests), the Benjamin Franklin State Dining Room, and the Thomas Jefferson State Reception Room, created from designs by Jefferson and Palladio. *Note:* You must write or phone in advance. *Tour Hours:* Mon-Fri, 9:30am, 10:30am, and 3:00pm. *Address:* 2201 C St., NW (202-647-3241). **M H T**

Treasury Building

The Treasury is one of the finest Greek Revival buildings in DC; it's certainly the largest. The building, which took three decades to complete, houses the Internal Revenue Service, the U.S. Mint, U.S. Customs, the Secret Service, and the Bureau of Alcohol, Tobacco, and Firearms. Public tours are limited, so prior reservations are a must. *Hours:* Sat, 10:00am-noon. *Address:* 1500 Pennsylvania Ave., NW (202-343-9136 or 377-9174). **M**

St. John's Church

Directly across from the White House, St. John's has long been known as the "Church of Presidents." Since James Madison established the precedent of presidential attendance, every President has worshipped at least once at St. John's. The "Presidents Windows" in the North Gallery honor six Presidents who were communicants of the Church. This distinctive DC landmark, with its graceful tower and columned portico, was the first building erected in the White House neighborhood and has been in use since 1816. *Hours:* daily, 9:00am-4:00pm. *Address:* 1525 H St., NW (202-347-8766) **M**

Octagon House

Despite its name, the Octagon House has just six sides. This handsome townhouse was built in 1800 by William Thornton, the architect of the Capitol. When British troops torched the White House in 1814, President Madison moved to the Octagon for six months while the Presidential mansion was rebuilt. Since 1898, the house has served as headquarters for the American Institute of Architects, who have restored and preserved it as a museum of architecture and decorative arts. *Hours:* Tues-Fri, 10:00am-4:00pm; Sat-Sun, 1:00pm-4:00pm. *Address:* 1799 New York Ave., NW (202-638-3105) **M T**

American Red Cross

The national headquarters of the American Red Cross is housed in a gleaming white edifice aptly called the "Marble Palace." Inside, you'll find displays and exhibits about the history and progress of the Red Cross, as well as some wonderful works of 19th- and 20th-century American art. Be sure to see the three Tiffany stained glass windows in the Governor's Hall. Young children will be interested in the doll and toy collection. *Hours:* Mon-Fri, 9:00am-4:00pm. *Address:* 431 17th St., NW (202-737-8300) **M H C T**

Federal Reserve Board

This building houses the administration of the Federal Reserve Board, which regulates national monetary policies. There are guided tours, a film presentation on the Fed, and a fine art gallery. *Hours:* Mon-Fri, 9:30am-4:00pm. *Address:* C St. between 20th & 21st Sts., NW (202-452-3149). **M T**

The John F. Kennedy Center

Kennedy Center for the Performing Arts

Located beside the Potomac River, the Kennedy Center is a grand building with three theaters, an opera house, and a symphony hall. Free guided tours provide a fascinating perspective on the opulent decor and controversial architecture. The views from the rooftop terraces are spectacular. *Hours:* open daily (tours 10:00am-1:00pm). *Address:* New Hampshire Ave. at F Street, NW (202-254-3600 or 254-3643). **M H T**

National Academy of Sciences

Established by an act of Congress in 1863, the National Academy of Sciences is an independent agency that advises Federal officials on scientific and technological matters. The Academy presents lively art exhibits and a free concert series. Don't miss the Albert Einstein Memorial created by Robert Berks to commemorate the centennial of the great scientist's birth. *Hours:* Mon-Fri, 9:00am-5:00pm. *Address:* 2101 Constitution Ave., NW (202-334-2439). **M H**

Truxton-Decatur Naval Museum

Situated in the carriage house of the old Stephen Decatur Mansion, this engaging museum focuses on the history of the Navy, Marines, Coast Guard, and Merchant Marine. Displays include ship models, antique firearms, medals, flags, photographs, and memorabilia of naval heroes. *Hours:* daily, 10:00am-4:00pm. *Address:* 1610 H St., NW. **M H**

AFL-CIO Building

You don't have to be a union member to appreciate the spectacular art displayed at the AFL-CIO headquarters. Foremost are the enormous murals by Lumen Winter—*Labor Is Life* and *Space Age*—both elaborate works in marble, glass, and gold. There are also interesting exhibits of union souvenirs and tools of labor in the lobby. *Hours:* daily, 9:00am-5:00pm. *Address:* 815 16th St., NW (202-637-5101). **M H**

Old Executive Office Building

Built in the ornate Second Empire style, with a mansard roof, pilasters, pillars, and porticos, this DC landmark has survived calls for redesign, remodeling, and demolition since its completion in 1888. The enormous interior outdoes the pompous facade with rich decoration bordering on the baroque. Originally housing the War, Navy, and State Departments, it now serves as office space for the White House staff and Presidential commissions. Closed to the public until 1985, the OEOB is now open for exclusive tours on Saturdays only. Highlights include the historic Indian Treaty Room and the East Rotunda. *Hours:* Sat, 9:00am-noon. (Phone for reservations Mon-Fri, 9:00am-noon.) *Address:* 17th St. & Pennsylvania Ave. (202-395-5895). **H T**

Downtown

FBI Headquarters

The FBI tour is one of DC's most popular attractions. An introductory film provides orientation for this fast-paced glimpse behind the scenes of the nation's premier law enforcement agency. The tour then proceeds through exciting exhibits that feature historic FBI cases, a visit to the state-of-the-art crime lab, and a bang-up finale when agents give a firearms demonstration. The one-hour tour is a big hit with children. *Hours:* Mon-Fri, 8:45am-4:15pm. *Address:* E St. between 9th & 10th Sts., NW (202-324-3447). **M H C T**

National Museum of American Art

Located in the Old Patent Building, the National Museum of American Art presents a comprehensive view of American arts from the Colonial era to the present. The permanent collection of 32,000 paintings, prints, drawings, sculpture, photos, and crafts includes works by Benjamin West, John Singer Sargent, Winslow Homer, Thomas Cole, Mary Cassatt, Man Ray, and Andrew Wyeth. Don't miss the grand Lincoln Gallery on the 3rd floor. With its high vaulted ceiling and marble pillars, this hall has earned the appellation "The Greatest Room in America." *Hours:* daily, 10:00am-5:30pm. *Address:* 8th & G Sts., NW (202-357-3176 or 357-3111). **M H T**

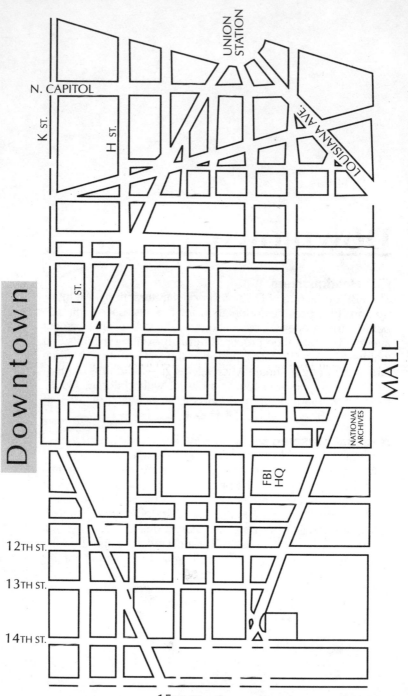

National Portrait Gallery

Sharing space in the Old Patent Building, the National Portrait Gallery serves as America's family album. Established by Congress, the Gallery honors people who have made significant contributions to U.S. history and culture. Highlights include Presidential portraits by Gilbert Stuart, John Singer Sargent, and Charles Peale, sculpture by Jo Davidson, the Galleries of American Leaders, the haunting photos by Mathew Brady in the Meserve Gallery, and the fabulous Great Hall on the 3rd floor. After a disastrous fire in 1877, the Hall was redecorated in flamboyant style with colorful stained glass and carved frescoes. *Hours:* daily, 10:00am-5:30pm. *Address:* 8th & F Sts., NW (202-357-2700). **M H T**

Ansel Adams Collection

There's a wonderful collection of Ansel Adams' most celebrated landscape photographs on permanent display at DC's Wilderness Society. *Hours:* Mon-Fri, 10:00am-5:00pm. *Address:* 900 17th St., NW (202-883-2300). **M H**

Ford's Theatre

Ford's Theatre has been faithfully restored to appear exactly as it did on the night of April 14, 1865, when President Lincoln was assassinated there by John Wilkes Booth. A moving museum in the basement chronicles Lincoln's life and death with audio-visual displays and memorabilia. *Hours:* daily, 9:00am-5:00pm. *Address:* 511 10th St., NW (202-426-6924). **M C T**

Petersen House

After visiting Ford's Theatre, cross the street to see Petersen House, where Lincoln was carried after being mortally wounded. The simple brick home has been restored and refurbished according to photos taken on the morning of April 15, 1865, when the President died there. Note the mantlepiece clock—it was stopped at 7:22, the time of Lincoln's death. *Hours:* daily, 9:00am-5:00pm. *Address:* 516 10th St., NW (202-426-6830). **M**

The Rotunda of the National Archives. (Photo: Stephen Brown)

National Archives

The National Archives is the repository for the three documents that form the foundation for American democracy: the Declaration of Independence, the Constitution, and the Bill of Rights. The Archives is also charged with the preservation of the government's documentary history. Along with hundreds of millions of reports, treaties, letters, photographs, maps, and documents, you'll find special exhibits, audio-visual presentations, and research facilities open to anyone interested in genealogy or historical research. *Hours:* daily, 10:00am-5:30pm. *Address:* 8th St. & Constitution Ave., NW (202-523-3000 or 523-3183). **M H T**

National Museum of Women in the Arts

Housed in an elegant Renaissance Revival building, this is the first major museum in the world devoted exclusively to women artists. Opened in 1987, its permanent collection and special shows focus on largely neglected paintings, sculpture, graphics, and textiles by women from the 14th century to the present. *Hours:* Tues-Sat, 10:00am-5:00pm; Sun, noon-5:00pm. *Address:* 1250 New York Ave., NW (202-783-5000). **M H T**

Union Station

Restored and rejuvenated, this monumental Beaux Arts building is much more than a train station. Designed by Daniel Burnham, Union Station combines the architectural grandeur of ancient Rome with the dynamism of turn-of-the-century America. The gargantuan interior now hosts hundreds of elegant shops, restaurants, and theaters. *Hours:* open 24 hours. *Address:* 40 Massachusetts Ave., NE (202-371-9441). **M H T**

National Building Museum

Devoted to architecture and interior design, this museum is located in one of DC's most extraordinary landmarks. The old Pension Building, designed by Civil War General Montgomery Meigis in 1881, is deceptively plain outside, but astonishing inside. It has been described as a cross between Diocletian's Baths and an Italian Renaissance palace. The majestic Great Hall has been the site of Inaugural Balls since Grover Cleveland's in 1885. *Hours:* Mon-Fri, 10:00am-4:00pm; Sat-Sun, noon-4:00pm. *Address:* F & G Sts. between 4th & 5th Sts., NW (202-272-2448). **M H T**

National Guard Heritage Gallery

This unusual exhibition center presents dramatic episodes from the history of America's citizen-soldiers. There are audio-visual programs focusing on Revolutionary War engagements, models of military aircraft, dioramas, weapons, and a sculpture garden. *Hours:* Mon-Fri, 9:00am-4:00pm. *Address:* Massachusetts Ave. & North Capitol St., NW. **M H C**

Jewish Historical Society

The Adas Israel Synagogue, a stately Federal-style building, serves as headquarters for DC's Jewish Historical Society and as a museum of Jewish life in the capital over the last two centuries. The restored sanctuary is especially lovely. *Hours:* Sun, 11:00am-3:00pm (or by appointment). *Address:* 701 3rd St., NW (202-789-0900). **M T**

National Theatre
Continually in operation at the same location since 1835, the National Theatre is one of America's oldest playhouses. Free guided tours of the renovated theater and backstage are conducted by appointment. *Hours:* Mon-Fri, 10:30am-4:30pm. *Address:* 1321 Pennsylvania Ave., NW (202-783-3370 or 628-6161). **M T**

Martin Luther King Jr Library
The MLK Library is DC's only building designed by the acclaimed architect Mies van der Rohe. This exciting institution is a dynamic cultural center with art galleries, free concert programs, a film series, children's events, an information service, the definitive Washingtoniana collection, a Black Studies Center, and much more. *Hours:* Mon-Thurs, 9:00am-9:00pm; Fri-Sat, 9:00am-5:30pm; Sun, 1:00pm-5:00pm. (Tours given Mon-Thurs, 9:00am-4:00pm.) *Address:* 901 G St., NW (202-727-1111). **M H C T**

Old Post Office
The Old Post Office, DC's best example of Victorian Romanesque architecture, has become a trendy marketplace filled with lively restaurants, shops, and entertainment venues. There are daily free events and tours year-round. The elegant clock tower, second only to the Washington Monument in height, provides terrific views of the capital. *Hours:* daily, 10:00am-9:30pm. *Address:* 1100 Pennsylvania Ave., NW (202-289-4224). **M H C T**

U.S. Navy Memorial
The "Lone Sailor" is dedicated to all who have served in the U.S. Navy since 1775. From May to September, the Navy Band and other military bands perform nightly concerts at the Memorial amphitheater. A Visitors Center adjacent to the Memorial completes the complex. *Hours:* open daily. *Address:* Pennsylvania Ave. between 7th & 9th Sts., NW (202-524-0830). **M H**

Washington Project for the Arts

The old F&W Grand Building is now home to an arts center dedicated to the DC avant-garde scene. The WPA is noted for its exciting performance pieces, video art, painting, and sculpture. *Hours:* Mon-Fri, 11:00am-6:00pm; Sat & Sun 11:00am-5:00pm. *Address:* 400 7th St., NW (202-347-8304). **M**

U.S. Department of Labor

The Frances Perkins Building features exhibits on the history of labor in America and four impressive murals by Jack Beal. *Hours:* Mon-Fri, 9:00am-4:30pm. *Address:* Constitution Ave. between 2nd & 3rd Sts., NW (202-523-4000). **M H**

New York Avenue Presbyterian Church

This historic church was attended by Presidents John Quincy Adams and Abraham Lincoln. The first draft of the Emancipation Proclamation and Lincoln's family pew are on display. The church is also noted for its contemporary stained glass windows. *Hours:* Tues-Sun, 9:00am-4:00pm. (Tours given Sun at 12:15pm.) *Address:* 1313 New York Ave., NW (202-393-3700). **M T**

Chinatown

Entry to DC's small Chinatown neighborhood is marked by a picturesque, authentic archway. Decorated in the classical Ming style and covered with dragons, the Friendship Arch commemorates the "sister city" relationship between Beijing and DC. The best time to visit Chinatown is February, when the Lunar New Year celebration brings dancers, floats, fireworks, bands, dragons, and parades to the district. *Hours:* open 24 hours. *Address:* G & H Sts. between 6th & 8th Sts., NW. **M C**

Free Room and Board

If you're short on cash but want to spend at least two weeks in DC, the Washington International Youth Hostel has an answer to your dilemma. In exchange for half a day of volunteer clerical work, the Hostel offers a bed plus a weekly food allowance. Openings exist year-round, but more positions are available during the summer season. To apply write: *AYH Volunteer Program, AYH National Office, PO Box 37613, Washington, DC 20013, USA.*

The National Postal Museum

A joint venture of the Smithsonian Institution and the U.S. Postal Service, the National Postal Museum is housed in an opulent Beaux Arts building next to Union Station. DC's newest museum brings to life 200 years of American history through interactive videos, hands-on displays, computer games, simulations, and other clever exhibits. Special galleries hold the most comprehensive collection of stamps in the world. *Hours:* daily, 10:00am-5:30pm. *Address:* Massachusetts Ave. and N. Capitol St., NE (202-633-9385). **M H C T**

Canadian Embassy

Facing the National Gallery across Pennsylvania Avenue, DC's finest post-modern building houses the new Canadian Embassy. This monumental marble edifice includes a gallery of Canadian art, a theater, a library, and a superb rotunda. *Hours:* Mon-Fri, 10:00am-5:00pm. *Address:* 501 Pennsylvania Ave., NW (202-682-1740). **M H T**

Northwest

National Geographic Society

The National Geographic Society's Explorers Hall celebrates a century of adventure, exploration, and education with exhibits on archaeology, space travel, world cultures, oceanography, geography, and more. Visitors of all ages will be challenged, entertained, and informed at this remarkable DC attraction. *Hours:* Mon-Sat, 9:00am-5:00pm; Sun, 10:00am-5:00pm. *Address:* 17th & M Sts., NW (202-857-7588). **M H C**

National Zoo

More than 3,000 animals—including giant pandas, blue-eyed tigers, Smokey the Bear, and pygmy hippopotami—reside at the National Zoological Park. Established by Congress a century ago, the National Zoo today covers 165 acres with modern habitats and exhibits. Be sure to see the Great Flight Cage, where visitors share a barrier-free environment with birds. Kids will love the Zoolab learning center with its captivating hands-on activities. *Hours:* daily, April 1-October 15, 8:00am-8:00pm; October 16-March 31, 8:00am-6:00pm. *Address:* 3000 block of Connecticut Ave., NW (202-673-4717 or 673-4955). **M H C T**

Anderson House

This spectacular mansion was once the home of Larz Anderson, a career diplomat who served as ambassador to Japan and Belgium. Today, Anderson House is the headquarters of the

Society of Cincinnati, the oldest patriotic organization in the United States, founded in 1783 by officers of the Continental Army. The first floor of the palatial residence contains an impressive collection of Revolutionary War relics and a portrait gallery. A grand marble stairway leads to the second floor, sumptuously decorated with Asian and European antiques. *Hours:* Tues-Sat, 1:00pm-4:00pm. *Address:* 2118 Massachusetts Ave., NW (202-785-0540). **M T**

Phillips Collection

Opened to the public in 1921, the Phillips Collection was America's first modern art museum. This exceptional gallery, housed in a lovely turn-of-the-century brownstone, is best known for its collections of French Impressionists, Post-Impressionists, and American Modernists. You'll find treasures by Renoir, Van Gogh, Cezanne, Klee, Degas, Monet, Matisse, Hopper, and many other greats. The Phillips also offers Sunday afternoon concerts. *Hours:* Tues-Sat, 10:00am-5:00pm; Sun, 2:00pm-7:00pm. *Address:* 1600 21st St., NW (202-387-0961). **M H T**

Washington Cathedral

Dominating DC's northwest skyline atop Mt. Albans, the neo-Gothic Washington Cathedral is one of the world's largest churches. In the grand tradition of medieval European cathedrals, the architects have incorporated flying buttresses, pinnacles, gargoyles, and stained glass. Make the most of your visit by taking the guided tour, where you'll see the Canterbury Pulpit, Rose Windows, the Crypt, and many chapels. The tour will also give you a greater understanding of the rich tradition of Gothic architecture. *Hours:* Mon-Sat, 10:00am-4:30pm; Sun, 8:00am-5:00pm. *Tours:* Mon-Sat, 10:00am-3:15pm; Sun, 1:00pm-2:00pm. *Address:* Wisconsin & Massachusetts Aves., NW (202-537-6200). **H T**

Rare Book Collection

Bibliophiles shouldn't miss the Washington Cathedral Rare Book Library. Works on display include an illuminated 1611 edition of the King James Bible, a first edition of the Book of Common Prayer published in 1549, and other priceless incunabula. *Hours:* Tues-Sat, noon-4:00pm. *Address:* Wisconsin & Massachusetts Aves., NW (202-537-6200).

Bishop's Garden

When visiting the Washington Cathedral, save time for a stroll in the serene Bishop's Garden. Entering through a 13th-century Norman archway, you'll discover a beautifully re-created medieval garden with stone-paved walkways, flowerbeds, carved niches, and tranquil pools. *Hours:* daily, 9:00am-6:00pm. *Address:* Wisconsin & Massachusetts Aves., NW (202-537-6200).

NRA Firearms Museum

Guns, guns, and more guns—nearly 2,000 of them—are on exhibit at the National Rifle Association's Firearms Museum. Displays range from primitive blunderbusses to modern laser-sight target pistols. *Hours:* daily, 10:00am-4:00pm. *Address:* 1600 Rhode Island Ave., NW (202-828-6194). **M**

Fondo Del Sol

An artist-directed gallery dedicated to promoting and preserving the arts and cultures of the Americas, the Fondo del Sol Visual Art Center presents exhibits of traditional and contemporary arts and crafts, concerts, performance art, poetry readings, and lectures. Every summer, Fondo del Sol sponsors a colorful Caribbean Festival. *Hours:* Wed-Sat, 12:30pm-5:30pm. *Address:* 2112 R St., NW (202-483-2777). **M H C**

Islamic Center

Visitors of all faiths are welcome at DC's magnificent Islamic Center and Mosque. The striking exterior is an amalgam of Middle Eastern and North African design styles. The interior provides illustration of the rich traditions of Islamic geometric art with lush Persian carpets, colorful Turkish tiles, and a spectacular Egyptian chandelier. Along with the Mosque, there's a museum, library, gift shop, and lecture hall, where educational programs on Islamic religion and culture are held. *Hours:* daily, 10:00am-5:00pm. *Address:* 2551 Massachusetts Ave., NW (202-332-8343). **M C T**

Washington Post

The *Washington Posts'* informative, hour-long tour provides a behind-the-scenes look at the production of the Capital's leading daily, from the printing plant to the newsroom. Reservations are essential. *Hours:* Mon-Fri, 10:00am-3:00pm. *Address:* 1150 15th St., NW (202-334-6000 or 334-7969). **M T**

Textile Museum

Housed in two adjoining historic homes, the Textile Museum presents an incomparable collection of textiles and rugs from around the world. Exhibitions have included Persian tribal carpets, pre-Columbian Mayan clothing, Ottoman Turkish embroideries, rare silks from southeast Asia, and Navajo blankets. This elegant museum's permanent collection has splendid examples of achievement in textile arts from Egypt to Indonesia. *Hours:* Tues-Sat, 10:00am-5:00pm; Sun, 1:00-5:00. *Address:* 2320 S St., NW (202-667-0441). **M T**

B'Nai B'Rith Museum

The B'Nai B'Rith Klutznick Museum offers a collection of Jewish ceremonial and folk art spanning 25 centuries and five continents. Hundreds of artifacts on display range from rare Babylonian coins to bilingual Indian prayerbooks written in Sanskrit and Hebrew. *Hours:* Sun-Fri, 10:00am-5:00pm. *Address:* 1640 Rhode Island Ave., NW (202-857-6583). **M H C T**

Armed Forces Medical Museum

This bizarre, fascinating museum began during the Civil War, when the Army's Surgeon General ordered the collection of "specimens of morbid anatomy." Since then, the collection has grown to specialize in pathology of disease, as well as war-related and everyday injuries. Displays include medical and surgical instruments, historic microscopes, shrunken heads, military projectiles, and a piece of Abraham Lincoln's skull. Not recommended for the squeamish or easily offended! *Hours:* Mon-Fri, 10:00am-5:30pm; Sat-Sun, noon-5:00pm. *Address:* 6825 16th St., NW (202-576-2418). **H T**

Barney Studio House

This turn-of-the-century gem, now a branch of the Smithsonian, was built by artist and patron Alice Pike Barney to be her home, studio, and salon. The Mediterranean-style villa is filled with Renaissance reproduction furniture, Tiffany glass, Oriental rugs, and art by Barney and her contemporaries. *Hours:* Wed, Thurs, & Sun, by appointment. *Address:* 2306 Massachusetts Ave., NW (202-357-3111). **H T**

Australian Embassy

The Australian Embassy Chancery building is one of the few DC diplomatic missions open to the general public, and there's an interesting exhibit of Australian crafts and products on display. Tours can also be arranged. *Hours:* Mon-Fri, 11:00am-3:00pm. *Address:* 1601 Massachusetts Ave., NW (202-797-3000). **H T**

Naval Observatory

Established in 1844, the U.S. Naval Observatory is the official source for standard time and astronomical data required for navigation at sea and in the air. The engaging hour-long tour includes a look at the cesium beam atomic clock and a peek through the century-old telescope used in the discovery of the moons of Mars. Special two-hour evening tours are held on Mondays at 8:30pm, and reservations are a must. *Hours:* Mon, 7:30pm-10:00pm. *Address:* Massachusetts Ave. at 34th St., NW (202-653-1543). **T C**

Scottish Rite Temple

John Russell Pope modeled this headquarters for the Scottish Rite of Freemasonry after the ruined tomb at Halicarnassus in Turkey, one of the Seven Wonders of the ancient world. The elaborate Temple is loaded with arcane symbols from the civilizations of antiquity and ornate decorations inside and out. The ceremonial rooms display architectural embellishments usually reserved for cathedrals or palaces. Other rooms exhibit regalia and memorabilia of such famous Masons as George Washington, General Douglas MacArthur, and astronaut Buzz Aldrin. *Hours:* Mon-Fri, 9:00am-4:00pm. *Address:* 1733 16th St., NW (202-232-3579). **M T**

Pierce Mill in Rock Creek Park
(Photo: Bill Clark/National Park Service)

48

Pierce Mill

Isaac Pierce built this overshot water mill on Rock Creek in 1820. For 70 years, wheat, corn, and rye were ground between the mill's great circular stones. The old mill has been restored and is back in the business of making flour and cornmeal. *Hours:* Wed-Sun, 9:00am-5:00pm. *Address:* Beach Dr. & Tilden St., NW (202-426-6908) **C T**

Art Barn Gallery

Housed in an early 19th-century carriage house, the Art Barn Gallery is devoted entirely to the works of local artists. Regular shows are supplemented by demonstrations in a variety of media each weekend. *Hours:* Wed-Sun, 10:00am-5:00pm. *Address:* 2401 Tilden St., NW (202-426-6719).

Rock Creek Park & Nature Center

Native Americans once lived along Rock Creek; later, settlers built cabins and mills along the boulder-strewn banks. Today, the park is a 1,700-acre recreation area with miles of hiking and riding trails, a golf course, tennis courts, picnic areas, a planetarium, and a nature center. Both self-guided and conducted nature walks are available. The Nature Center, at 5200 Glover Rd., is especially interesting for children. *Park Hours:* daily, 7:00am-dusk. *Nature Center Hours:* Tues-Sun, 9:00am-5:00pm. *Planetarium Hours:* Sat-Sun, 1:00pm-4:00pm. *Address:* Military Rd., NW (202-426-6834 or 426-6829). **H C T**

National Housing Center

The National Association of Home Builders presents exhibits on international housing development, home design, and architecture at DC's National Housing Center. *Hours:* Tues-Sat, 10:00am-4:00pm. *Address:* 15th & M Sts., NW (202-822-0200). **M H**

Bethune Museum Archives

Housed in a Victorian rowhouse, the Bethune Museum Archives commemorates the noted black educator Mary McLeod Bethune. The museum offers regular exhibitions on black history and the Civil Rights Movement. The old carriage house behind the museum is now home to the National Archives for Black Women's History. *Hours:* Tues-Sat, 10:00am-4:00pm. *Address:* 1318 Vermont Ave., NW (202-332-1233). **M T**

St. Mary's Episcopal Church

James Renwick, architect of New York's St. Patrick's Cathedral, created this pure Victorian Gothic replica of an English village church in 1886. Inside this lovely brick church, Renwick lavished extraordinary attention on the design and decoration of furnishings: the pews are hand-carved oak, the walls are decorated with colorful stenciled designs, and the stained glass windows are from Tiffany. *Hours:* Mon-Fri, 9:00am-2:00pm. *Address:* 728 23rd St., NW (202-333-3985). **M**

Japanese Embassy Garden

Lovely formal gardens are hidden behind the Georgian style Japanese Embassy. Within the gardens, you'll discover an ancient teahouse, imported from Japan in 1960 to commemorate the Treaty of Friendship between Japan and the U.S. *Hours:* May-October, by appointment. *Address:* 2520 Massachusetts Ave., NW (202-939-6700). **T**

Watkins Gallery

American University hosts the Watkins Art Gallery, which presents changing exhibitions of contemporary art and selections from a permanent collection of American art. *Hours:* Mon-Fri, 10:00am-4:00pm. *Address:* 4400 Massachusetts Ave., NW (202-885-1670) .

St. Paul's & Rock Creek Cemetery

Dating to 1712, St. Paul's is DC's oldest standing church. (The present Colonial-style building is a 1921 restoration.) Nearby, the Rock Creek Cemetery, the resting place of many famous Washingtonians, is best known for the moving Adams Memorial. The six-foot bronze figure by Auguste Saint-Gaudins is commonly called "Grief" after a remark by Mark Twain that the sculpture embodied all of human grief. *Hours:* Mon-Fri, 8:30am-4:30pm; Sat, 8:30am-1:00pm. *Address:* Rock Creek Church Rd. & Webster Rd., NW (202-829-0585).

Fort Stevens

On July 11, 1864, 20,000 Confederate troops under the command of General Jubal Early attacked Fort Stevens. Eager to observe Federal soldiers in action, President Lincoln watched the battle from a parapet. Legend has it that Lincoln came under Rebel fire and had to be pulled to safety by an officer.

Today, the ramparts, earthworks, and gun emplacements have been meticulously restored. *Hours:* open 24 hours. *Address:* 13th St. & Fort Stevens Dr., NW (202-426-6829). **C T**

International Visitors Information Service
The IVIS is a non-profit organization created to help the foreign traveler make the most of a visit to DC. The center provides multilingual information on sightseeing, cultural and sporting events, and accommodations, plus free maps. The IVIS also offers volunteer language assistants to aid non-English-speaking tourists. *Hours:* Mon-Fri, 9:00am-5:00pm. *Address:* 733 15th St., NW (202-783-6540). **M**

Meridian House
This 20th-century version of an 18th-century French chateau was designed by John Russell Pope, architect of the Jefferson Memorial and the National Archives. Since 1960, Meridian House has been home to the Washington International Center, a non-profit organization that maintains this meeting place for visitors and diplomats, promotes cultural exchange programs, and presents international art exhibits. *Hours:* daily, 1:00pm-5:00pm. *Address:* 1630 Crescent Place, NW (202-667-6800).

Saint Sophia Cathedral
Built in 1956, Saint Sophia Cathedral is the largest Greek Orthodox Church in the United States. The Cathedral's chief distinction is its extraordinary Byzantine-style artwork. The mosaics and murals throughout the church depict a celestial hierarchy replete with hosts of seraphim and Old Testament prophets. It's possible to visit the Cathedral during daily services, but guided tours must be arranged in advance. *Hours:* daily (call for times of services and tours). *Address:* Massachusetts Ave. at 36th St., NW (202-333-4730). **H T**

Howard Gallery of Fine Arts
Howard University's Gallery of Fine Arts presents exhibitions of contemporary American and international art, as well as a permanent collection of African art. *Hours:* Mon-Fri, 9:30am-4:30pm; Sun, 1:00pm-4:00pm. *Address:* 2455 6th St., NW (202-636-6100).

IMF Visitors' Center

Located in the world headquarters of the multilateral development bank, the International Monetary Fund Visitors' Center presents shows by international artists, a permanent art exhibit from its own collection, diverse cultural events, a film series, an economic forum, seminars, Third World crafts, and a daily showing of the film *The IMF at Work. Hours:* Mon-Fri, 9:30am-6:00pm. *Address:* 700 19th St., NW (202-623-6869). **M T**

Khalil Gibran Memorial Garden

This serene two-acre garden honors the Lebanese poet Khalil Gibran, whose verses on love, peace, and compassion inspire people all around the world. The Islamic-style garden surrounds a tranquil fountain court and a bust of the author. *Hours:* open 24 hours. *Address:* 3100 Massachusetts Ave., NW. **H**

Art Club of Washington

Occupying two historic houses, the Art Club of Washington has a mission to preserve the arts of the Capital. The upper floors house a permanent exhibition of 19th- and 20th-century art, plus Georgian period furnishings, while the lower galleries present monthly shows featuring contemporary art. The main building was James Monroe's Executive Mansion for a short time. *Hours:* Tues-Fri, 2:00pm-5:00pm; Sat, 10:00am-2:00pm; Sun, 1:00pm-5:00pm. *Address:* 2017 I St., NW (202-331-7282). **M**

Citadel Motion Picture and Video Center

This massive Art Deco-style complex—originally a bowling alley and roller rink—has been converted into a film and video production facility, open for tours upon request. *Address:* 1649 Kalorama Rd., NW (202-667-0344). **C T**

St. Matthew's Cathedral

This Italianate, Renaissance-style Roman Catholic cathedral is worth a visit for its richly decorated interior, shimmering with colorful mosaics, vibrant frescos, and candle-lit chapels. However, most tourists visit because Pres. John F. Kennedy worshipped in the church, and his funeral mass was held there November 25, 1963. *Hours:* daily, 6:30am-6:30pm (tours Sun 2:30pm-4:30pm). *Address:* 1725 Rhode Island Ave., NW (202-347-3215). **M T**

Northeast

Franciscan Monastery
Visitors of all faiths will long remember a tour of the century-old Franciscan Monastery. The Byzantine-style church and grounds re-create many famous shrines of ancient Israel and medieval Europe. Included are replicas of the manger at Bethlehem, the grotto of Nazareth, the Holy Sepulcher, the grotto of Lourdes, and the Portiuncula Chapel, where St. Francis established his order in the 13th century. Under the church, there's a somewhat bizarre reproduction of the early Christian catacombs of Rome. Over 40 acres of gardens surround the Monastery. *Hours:* Mon-Sat, 8:30am-5:00pm; Sun, 1:00pm-4:00pm. *Address:* 1400 Quincy St., NE (202-526-6800). **M H C T**

Kenilworth Aquatic Gardens
More than 100,000 flowering water plants, including lotuses, lilies, hyacinths, and bamboo, thrive in ponds and marshes along the Anacostia River. There's a floral extravaganza from May through early fall. To enjoy the gardens at their best, visit in the morning. *Hours:* daily, 7:00am-dusk. *Address:* Kenilworth Ave. & Douglas St., NE (202-426-6905).

National Arboretum
Spring is the peak season for a visit to the 444-acre National Arboretum, when the hillsides are ablaze with azaleas, wildflowers, magnolias, boxwoods, and cherry trees. During the summer, roses, rhododendrons, herbs, and peonies proliferate. The fall foliage is spectacular, and winter is the season for hollies and evergreens. Don't overlook the National Herb Garden and the charming Japanese Garden and bonsai collection, a bicentennial gift from the people of Japan. *Hours:* Mon-Fri,

53

The National Arboretum

8:00am-5:00pm; Sat-Sun, 10:00am-5:00pm. *Address:* 3501 New York Ave., NE (202-475-4815). **H**

National Shrine

The National Shrine of the Immaculate Conception is the largest Roman Catholic church in North America and the seventh largest in the world. Of Byzantine, Romanesque, and contemporary design, with elaborate mosaic, carvings, tile work, and sculpture, the Shrine provides a dramatic counterpoint to DC's civic architecture. A Byzantine-style dome crowns the interior, which seats more than 3,000 people and has 56 chapels. Monday through Saturday, guided tours begin at the Memorial Hall every half hour from 9:00am to 4:00pm (Sunday, 1:30pm-4:00pm). *Hours:* April-Oct: daily, 7:00am-7:00pm; Nov-March: daily, 7:00am-6:00pm. *Address:* 4th St. & Michigan Ave., NE (202-526-8300). **M T**

Gallaudet University

Established in 1864, Gallaudet is the world's only accredited university for the deaf. The beautiful neo-Gothic campus was designed by Frederick Law Olmsted and Calvert Vaux. You can arrange for a tour of the campus at the Visitor's Center, where you'll also find a multi-media exhibit. *Hours:* Mon-Fri, 9:00am-4:00pm. *Address:* 800 Florida Ave., NE (202-651-4000 or TTY 651-5359). **T H**

Southeast

Cedar Hill
This lovely Victorian house, with its wonderful views across the Anacostia of DC, was home to the renowned abolitionist and orator Frederick Douglass from 1877 until his death in 1895. The National Park Service has restored Cedar Hill with its original furnishings, library, art, and Douglass' memorabilia. The guided tour presents a moving portrait of "The Father of the Civil Rights Movement." *Hours:* daily, 9:00am-4:00pm. *Address:* 1411 W St., SE (202-426-5961). **C T**

Congressional Cemetery
Since 1807, Christ Church Cemetery has served as an unofficial burial place for members of Congress and other prominent citizens. Among the distinguished internees are Elbridge Gerry, signer of the Declaration of Independence and Vice President under Madison, John Philip Sousa, and Choctaw Chief Pushmataha. Eighty of the gravesites are marked by odd looking cenotaphs designed by Benjamin Latrobe, one of the U.S. Capitol's chief architects. The gatekeeper can provide a map of the memorial sites. *Hours:* daily, 7:30am-3:30pm. *Address:* 1801 E St., SE. **M**

Washington Navy Yard
Opened in 1799, the Washington Navy Yard is the oldest continuously used naval installation in the U.S. Originally a shipyard for the fledgling navy, it later became a manufacturing

55

facility for weapons and munitions. Since the 1960's, the yard has been used mainly for administrative functions. Visitors are free to roam around and see the old military and industrial buildings, built mostly between 1800 and 1900. There's also an outdoor military history park with 18th-, 19th-, and 20th-century cannons and naval artifacts. At the docks, you can explore the *U.S.S. Barry*, a retired Navy destroyer. *Hours:* Mon-Fri, 9:00am-4:00pm; Sat-Sun, 10:00am-5:00pm. *Address:* 9th & M St., SE (202-433-2651 or 433-3377). **M H C T**

Navy Memorial Museum

Housed in an immense 19th-century warehouse, the Navy Memorial Museum traces the history of the U.S. Navy from the Revolutionary War to the Space Age. Thousands of artifacts, including 18th-century deck guns, midget submarines, anti-aircraft guns, ship models, flags, airplanes, and much more, are on display. The Visitors Center presents an informative audiovisual show. During the summer months, the Navy Band performs a nautical show and concert every Wednesday evening at 8:45pm. *Hours:* Mon-Fri, 9:00am-4:00pm; Sat-Sun, 10:00am-5:00pm. *Address:* 9th & M Sts., SE (202-433-2651; 433-2678 for concert info). **M H C**

Eastern Market

Designed in 1871 by Adolph Cluss, architect of the Smithsonian Arts and Industries Building, the delightful Eastern Market is an enduring DC institution. In the tradition of European market arcades, the Eastern Market is the 19th-century equivalent of the supermarket; you can find everything from fresh eggs to homemade cannoli. The best time to visit is on Saturdays, when the Market really bustles and vendors set up extra stands. *Hours:* Tues-Thurs., 7:00am-6:00pm; Fri-Sat, 6:00am-7:00pm. *Address:* 7th St. between North Carolina & C St., SE (202-544-5646). **M C**

Anacostia Museum

This branch of the Smithsonian Institution, located in the historic Anacostia district, presents exhibitions on the culture and history of African-Americans, contemporary urban problems, jazz, photography, and African art. The museum also provides a venue for free concerts, poetry readings, plays, and dance. *Hours:* daily, 10:00am-5:00pm. *Address:* 1901 Fort Place, SE (202-287-3369). **H C T**

Marine Corps Museum

The Marine Corps Museum, housed in a restored 19th-century barrack, explores two centuries of fighting tradition with displays of weapons, uniforms, flags, models, memorabilia, and equipment. There's also a special collection on military music, with mementos of John Philip Sousa, who served as the Marine Corps Bandmaster. *Hours:* Mon-Sat, 10:00am-4:00pm; Sun, noon-5:00pm. *Address:* 9th & M Sts., SE (202-433-3840). **M H C**

Sunset Parade

Friday evenings throughout the summer, the Marine Corps Band, Drum and Bugle Corps, Color Guard, and Silent Drill Team present an impressive military pageant at the historic Marine Barracks Quadrangle. Reservations are a must for this popular DC spectacle. *Hours:* May-Sept: Fri, 8:20pm. *Address:* 8th & I Sts., SE (202-433-6060). **M H C**

Southwest

Bureau of Engraving and Printing
The Bureau of Engraving and Printing produces all paper currency, postage stamps, Treasury bonds, food stamps, certificates, and revenue documents issued by the Federal government. Highlights of the popular self-guided tour include the currency production operation—from paper to finished greenbacks—and the complex intaglio process for printing postage stamps. *Hours:* Mon-Fri, 9:00am-2:00pm. *Address:* 14th & C Sts., SW (202-447-9709). **M H T**

Voice of America
The Voice of America is the worldwide radio network of the International Communications Agency. Its task is to dispense objectively reported news throughout the world and to promote American-style democracy. Broadcasts are beamed 24 hours a day in Russian, Mandarin, Serbo-Croatian, and 37 other languages. The guided tour includes a visit to a live radio broadcast. *Hours:* Mon-Fri, 8:30am-3:30pm. *Address:* 330 Independence Ave., SW (202-485-6231). **M H T**

Lightship *Chesapeake*
The decommissioned Coast Guard lightship *Chesapeake* is now a floating ecological workshop. Hands-on displays and activities focus on marine biology, pollution, navigation, and estuary management. Park Service guides utilize on-board labs and an aquarium stocked with Potomac River species to pre-

58

sent educational programs. *Hours:* Tues, Thurs, & Sat, 1:00pm-4:00pm. *Address:* 1200 Ohio Dr., SW (202-426-6896). **C T**

East Potomac Park

East Potomac Park occupies a man-made peninsula between the Potomac River and the Washington Channel directly south of the Jefferson Memorial. Along with recreational activities, you'll find the National Park Service HQ Visitor Center, where you can get information on dozens of monuments, buildings, and parks under Park Service management. Don't overlook East Potomac's newest attraction: Seward Johnson's astonishing sculpture *The Awakening*, a gargantuan figure that seems to be emerging from the earth. *Hours:* daily, dawn to dusk. *Address:* Ohio Dr., SW (202-426-6792). **H C**

U.S. Postal Service

Philatelists shouldn't miss the U.S. Postal Service Philatelic Center. This small exhibit shows both regularly available issues and rare stamps. *Hours:* Mon-Fri, 9:00am-4:30pm. *Address:* L'Enfant Plaza West, SW (202-245-2000). **M H**

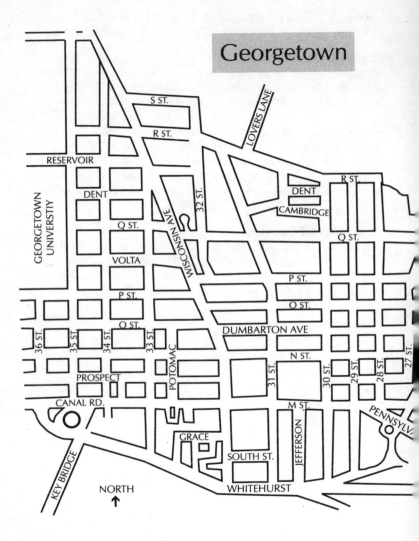

Georgetown

S ST.
R ST.
LOVERS LANE
RESERVOIR
DENT
CAMBRIDGE
R ST.
GEORGETOWN UNIVERSTIY
DENT
Q ST.
32 ST.
WISCONSIN AVE
VOLTA
Q ST.
P ST.
P ST.
O ST.
O ST.
DUMBARTON AVE
36 ST.
35 ST.
34 ST.
33 ST.
POTOMAC
N ST.
31 ST.
30 ST.
29 ST.
28 ST.
27 ST.
PROSPECT
CANAL RD.
M ST.
JEFFERSON
PENNSYLV.
GRACE
SOUTH ST.
KEY BRIDGE
NORTH
↑
WHITEHURST

60

Georgetown

Old Stone House

Built in 1765, this unpretentious dwelling is DC's oldest surviving pre-Revolutionary house. Originally the home and workshop of a cabinetmaker, it has been restored and furnished with items typical of a late 18th-century middle-class household. Guides in period dress demonstrate Colonial crafts such as spinning, weaving, candlemaking, and sewing, and they lead candlelight tours on Wednesday evenings. *Hours:* Wed-Sun, 9:30am-5:00pm. *Address:* 3051 M St., NW (202-426-6851). **C T**

Dumbarton Oaks

This marvelous 19th-century estate is one of DC's special treasures. The stately mansion, where conferences that laid the groundwork for the United Nations were held, is surrounded by lavish formal gardens. Inside you'll find the greatest collection of Byzantine art in North America, as well as a superb display of pre-Columbian art from Latin America. Don't miss the historic Music Room, with Italian, French, and Flemish Renaissance furnishings. *House Hours:* Tues-Sun, 2:00pm-5:00pm. *Garden Hours:* Tues-Sun, 2:00pm-6:00pm (Note: free November-April only.) *Address:* 1703 32nd St., NW (202-338-8278). **T**

Dumbarton House

Dumbarton House, one of DC's finest early Federal-style houses, serves as the headquarters for the National Society of Colonial Dames of America. The restored brick mansion has been furnished with antiques from 1780 to 1810. The collections of early American porcelain, crystal, silver, and jewelry are noteworthy. *Hours:* Mon-Sat, 9:00am-12:30pm. *Address:* 2715 Q St., NW (202-337-2288). **T**

Spectrum Gallery
This cooperative gallery is operated by 30 DC artists. Changing displays include sculpture, paintings, ceramics, jewelry, graphics, and textile arts. *Hours:* Tues-Sat, 10:00am-5:00pm; Sun, 2:00pm-5:00pm. *Address:* 1132 29th St., NW (202-333-0954).

Chesapeake & Ohio Canal
Built between 1828 and 1850, the C & O Canal extended from Georgetown to Cumberland, Maryland—185 miles west. Now maintained by the National Park Service, it remains one of the most authentic 19th-century canals in the country. You can hike, bike, canoe, or just stroll along the old towpath and enjoy Georgetown's rich architectural heritage. During the summer, free concerts are held on the C & O at 30th and Jefferson Sts. For information on concerts and other C & O Park events, call 202-484-0275. **C T**

St. John's Church
Established in 1796, St. John's Episcopal is the oldest church in Georgetown. It was designed by William Thornton, architect of the Capitol Building, and Francis Scott Key was a founding member of the congregation. *Hours:* daily, 9:00am-5:00pm. *Address:* 3240 O St., NW (202-338-1796).

Renwick Chapel
Designed by James Renwick, who also did the Smithsonian Castle, the Oak Hill Cemetery Chapel is a gem of Victorian Gothic Revival architecture. Established in 1849, Oak Hill Cemetery is filled with marvelous monuments, sculpture, iron benches, and carved markers. *Hours:* daily, 8:00am-5:00pm. *Address:* R St. & 29th St., NW (202-337-2835).

Tudor Place

William Thornton also designed this handsome Federal-style mansion in 1794 for Martha Parke Curtis, granddaughter of Martha Washington. The house is open for tours by reservation only. *Hours:* Tue-Sat. *Address:* 1644 31st St., NW (202-965-0400). **T**

Georgetown University

Founded in 1789, Georgetown University is the oldest Roman Catholic college in the United States. Guided tours provide an insider's view of the University's eclectic architecture and impressive art treasures. *Hours:* Mon-Sat, 9:00am-4:00pm (tours by appointment). *Address:* 37th & O Sts., NW (202-687-3634). **T**

Trolley Tours

Rest your feet and get a free sightseeing tour of the district on the Georgetown Trolley. You can catch this motorized replica of an old streetcar at numerous stops indicated by distinctive green and white signs. It's also possible to board across the Potomac at the Rosslyn Metro station. *Hours:* Tues-Sat, 10:30am-3:30pm. For information, call 202-333-3577.

Arlington, VA

Arlington National Cemetery
Since its establishment in 1864, Arlington has become the nation's official burial ground, where both the great and the ordinary who served the U.S. in every war and military action are interred. It is the final resting place for such illustrious figures as General John J. Pershing, boxing champ Joe Louis, astronauts Grissom and Chaffee, Oliver Wendell Holmes, and John Foster Dulles. The most visited sites at Arlington are the Tomb of the Unknown Soldier and the Kennedy Memorials. *Hours:* daily, 8:00am-7:00pm. *Address:* Memorial Bridge (703-692-0931). **M T**

Arlington House
The grandeur and tragedy of DC history come together at this classic Greek Revival mansion, originally the home of George Washington Park Curtis, grandson of Martha Washington, and later the home of General Robert E. Lee. During the Civil War, Arlington House was confiscated by Union troops, who used it as an army camp and military cemetery. Until 1925, the mansion served as headquarters for the National Cemetery. In 1955, it was designated as a memorial to Robert E. Lee. Many original furnishings have been returned, and the mansion is being restored to its antebellum appearance. *Hours:* daily, 9:30am-4:30pm (Oct-March); daily, 9:30am-6:00pm (April-Sept). *Address:* Arlington National Cemetery (703-285-2598). **M T**

Marine Corps Memorial

The Marine Corps Memorial depicts the famous flag-raising on Iwo Jima on Feb. 25, 1945. Inspired by the Pulitzer Prize-winning photograph by Joe Rosenthal, the Iwo Jima Monument is dedicated to all Marines who died in battle since 1775. During the summer, the Marine Drum and Bugle Corps and Color Guard present a formal sunset ceremony and parade at the memorial on Tuesday evenings at 7:00pm. *Address:* North Meade & Fairfax Dr., Arlington National Cemetery (703-285-2598). **M**

Netherlands Carillon

The Netherlands Carillon, an expression of gratitude from the Dutch people for U.S. aid during and after World War II, is an enduring symbol of friendship between the two nations. The 49-bell carillon is housed in a dramatic steel tower set on a quartzite plaza. Concerts by international carillonneurs are presented each Saturday from April through August. *Hours:* daily, 8:00am-7:00pm. *Address:* Arlington National Cemetery, North Entrance (703-285-2598). **M**

The Pentagon

Headquarters of the U.S. Department of Defense, the Pentagon is the world's largest office building. Virtually a city in itself, the Pentagon houses more than 25,000 civilian and military employees along 17.5 miles of corridors. To see the enormous building, you must join the hour-long guided tour. As an introduction, you'll see the 15-minute film "History of the Pentagon." *Hours:* Mon-Fri, 9:30am-3:30pm. *Address:* off Interstate 395 (202-695-1776). **M H T**

Theodore Roosevelt Island

Theodore Roosevelt Island is a fitting memorial to the first environmentalist President. Although the 88-acre island in the Potomac is within sight of DC, it remains a wilderness reserve of woods, marsh, and swamp, and home to a wide variety of wildlife. Free conducted nature walks are available on weekends during warm weather months. *Hours:* daily, dawn to dusk. *Address:* Lee Highway at North Lynne St. (703-285-2600). **C T**

Arlington Historical Museum

This local history museum contains an amusing jumble of memorabilia, costumes, Confederate artifacts, Indian relics, Colonial furnishings, and historical odds and ends. *Hours:* Fri-Sat, 11:00am-3:00pm; Sun, 2:00pm-5:00pm. *Address:* 1805 S. Arlington Ridge Rd. (703-892-4204).

Visitors Center

The Arlington Visitors Center, located near Crystal City in South Arlington, provides free maps, brochures, guides, and sightseeing information. *Hours:* Mon-Sat, 9:00am-5:00pm; Sun, 10:00am-4:00pm. *Address:* 735 S. 18th St. (703-358-5720).

Art Center

The Arlington Art Center offers diverse exhibitions by local, national, and international artists. Recent shows have included multimedia constructions by Hector Almodovar and paintings by Anne Handcock. *Hours:* Tues-Sat,11:00am-5:00pm. *Address:* 3550 Wilson Blvd. (703-524-1494). **M H**

Gulf Branch Nature Center

The focus here is on environmental appreciation and understanding. You'll find live animal displays, exhibits on forestry, conservation, weather, geology, and local plant life, as well as restored 19th-century homes and craftshops. *Hours:* Tues-Sat, 9:00am-5:00pm; Sun, 1:00pm-5:00pm. *Address:* 3608 Military Rd. (703-358-3403 or 558-2340). **C T**

Columbia Island

A large area of Columbia Island has been designated as Lady Bird Johnson Park in honor of the First Lady who did so much to beautify America. Thousands of dogwoods and millions of daffodils, tulips, and roses have been planted around the island. In the center of the park is the Lyndon Johnson Memorial. Landscaped gardens and walkways surround a simple red granite monument for the 36th President. At the southern tip of the island, you'll find the Navy Marine Memorial, created by Earnesto del Piatta in 1934, one of DC's loveliest and least-known monuments. *Hours:* daily, dawn to dusk. *Address:* George Washington Memorial Parkway.

Long Branch Nature Center

Visitors to this nature center enjoy guided nature hikes, photo safaris, a wildflower garden, wild marshlands, and special astronomy programs. *Hours:* Tues-Sat, 10:00am-5:00pm; Sun, 1:00pm-5:00pm. *Address:* 625 S. Carlin Springs Rd. (703-671-7716 or 358-6535). **C T**

George Mason Gallery

George Mason University Gallery presents changing exhibitions featuring DC-area photographers, sculptors, painters, and textile artists, as well as international shows. *Hours:* Mon-Fri, 9:00am-9:00pm. *Address:* 3401 N. Fairfax Dr. (703-841-2604). **M**

Gateway Park

Arlington's newest park is a showcase for special events, such as music concerts, art exhibits, magic shows, horticultural displays, and much more. *Hours:* daily, 8:00am-dusk. *Address:* 300 Lee Highway (703-358-3320). **M C**

WETA Television Studio

WETA, DC's public broadcasting station, offers an interesting tour of its studios, control rooms, and production facilities. *Hours:* Mon-Fri, 10:00am-2:00pm (tours by appointment only). *Address:* 3620 27th St. (703-998-2697). **C T**

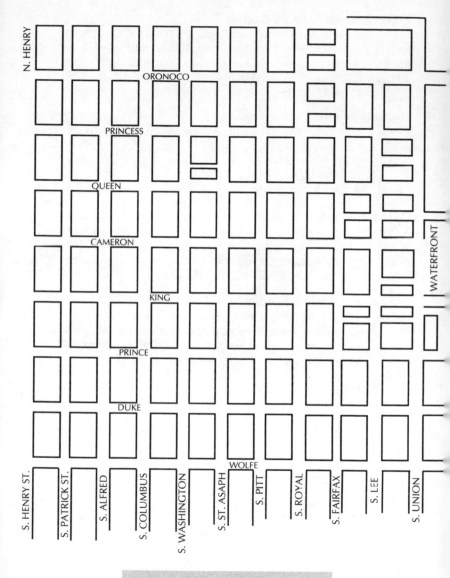

ORONOCO

PRINCESS

QUEEN

CAMERON

KING

PRINCE

DUKE

WOLFE

N. HENRY

WATERFRONT

S. HENRY ST.

S. PATRICK ST.

S. ALFRED

S. COLUMBUS

S. WASHINGTON

S. ST. ASAPH

S. PITT

S. ROYAL

S. FAIRFAX

S. LEE

S. UNION

Alexandria, VA

Alexandria, VA

Ramsey House

This historic home, built in 1724 by Alexandria's first mayor, should be your first stop in town, because it now serves as Alexandria's Visitors Center. The helpful staff will provide free parking passes, maps, a walking tour brochure, a calendar of events, and guides to local attractions, lodging, galleries, and shops. *Hours:* daily, 9:00am-5:00pm. *Address:* 221 King St. (703-8384200). **T M**

Stabler-Leadbeater Apothecary

Founded in 1792 by Edward Stabler, the apothecary remained in business until 1932, through five generations of his family. Now a museum, it preserves a colorful 200-year old collection of glassware, antique pharmaceutical supplies, and the shop's original furnishings. Prescription books indicate that George Washington, Daniel Webster, Henry Clay, and Robert E. Lee were customers. *Hours:* Mon-Sat, 10:00am-4:00pm; Sun, noon-5:00pm. *Address:* 107 S. Fairfax St. (703-836-3713).

Athenaeum

This imposing Greek Revival building was built as a bank in 1851. Today, the North Virginia Fine Arts Association uses it as a gallery and center for art shows, concerts, films, and lectures. *Hours:* Tues-Sat, 10:00am-4:00pm; Sun, 1:00pm-4:00pm. *Address:* 201 Prince St. (703-548-0035).

George Washington Masonic National Memorial

George Washington Masonic Memorial

Built by the Freemasons of America to honor the first Master of
the Alexandria Lodge, this remarkable edifice is modeled on
the ancient lighthouse of Alexandria, Egypt. Towering 331 feet
above the town on Shooter's Hill, it affords marvelous views of
the DC area. The museum contains a wide range of Washington memorabilia, including the President's family Bible, a
clock from Mt. Vernon that stopped at the time of his death,
and the trowel he used in laying the Capitol cornerstone in
1793. Along with other Washington relics, murals, and diora-

mas, there are unusual mementos such as the handcuffs used on John Brown, a chip off Plymouth Rock, and arcane Masonic regalia. *Hours:* daily, 9:00am-5:00pm. *Address:* 101 Callahan Dr., off King St. (703-683-2007). **M C T**

Christ Church

Built in 1773, Christ Church remains a fine example of Colonial ecclesiastical architecture. The late-Georgian church is trimmed with white stone from the same quarry that supplied the Capitol Building. The only exterior alteration was the 1818 addition of a belfry and cupola. Inside, original features include pews used by the Washington and Lee families. Christ Church Cemetery is the resting place for many of Alexandria's early residents and Confederate soldiers who died in city hospitals during the Civil War. *Hours:* Mon-Sat, 9:00am-4:00pm; Sun, 2:00pm-5:00pm. *Address:* 118 N. Washington St. (703-549-1450). **M**

Friendship Fire Company

Though this historic building has been closed to the public for a few years, the City of Alexandria has plans to re-open the museum of historic fire-fighting equipment and memorabilia soon. The volunteer fire company has quite a past—George Washington was a founding member. Among the prized possessions is a French-built fire engine donated by Washington in 1775. The fire station, a charming Victorian building, was completed in 1855. Contact the Alexandria Convention & Visitors Bureau for more information. *Address:* 107 S. Alfred St. **C**

Lyceum

Established in 1839 as a cultural and scientific center, the Lyceum remains a graceful example of Greek Revival architecture. During the Civil War, it served as a hospital and later as a private residence and a library. It now houses an interpretive center for the history of Virginia from Colonial days to the present. There are audio-visual presentations, paintings, antiques, maps, and local artifacts. *Hours:* daily, 10:00am-5:00pm. *Address:* 201 S. Washington St. (703-838-4994).

Old Presbyterian Meeting House

This unadorned brick church, erected in 1744 by Scottish settlers, was a gathering place for Virginia patriots and Revolutionary War heroes. The Tomb of the Unknown Soldier of the American Revolution is in a quiet corner of the church cemetery. *Hours:* Mon-Fri, 9:00am-4:00pm. *Address:* 321 S. Fairfax St. (703-549-6670) .

Torpedo Factory Arts Center

Once used as a munitions factory, the Arts Center is now studio and gallery space for 200 professional artists and craftspeople. The massive complex, covering an entire city block, overlooks Alexandria's historic waterfront. Along with the weavers, potters, jewelers, printers, sculptors, and painters, you'll find an engaging urban archaeology program and numerous exhibitions. *Hours:* daily, 10:00am-5:00pm. *Address:* 105 N. Union St. (703-838-4565).

Fort Ward

Fort Ward Historic Site is one of the best remaining examples of DC's Civil War defenses. Reconstructed from Mathew Brady's photographs, Fort Ward is a 40-acre complex with earthwork bastions, officer's quarters, camp headquarters, and a museum with an extensive collection of Civil War memorabilia. Special events at the fort include summer evening concerts, battle re-enactments, living history displays, and lectures. *Park Hours:* daily, 9:00am-dusk. *Museum Hours:* Tues-Sat, 9:00am-5:00pm; Sun, noon-5:00pm. *Address:* 4301 W. Braddock Rd. (703-838-4848 or 750-6425). **C T**

Lloyd House

This fine specimen of Georgian architecture was built in 1797 by John Wise and acquired by the Lloyd family in 1832. It houses a comprehensive collection of books, documents, maps, and genealogical records relating to the history of Alexandria and northern Virginia. Alexandria's original 18th-century library is also on display. *Hours:* Mon-Fri, 10:00am-6:00pm. *Address:* 220 N. Washington St. (703-838-4577).

Waterfront Museum

The Alexandria Waterfront Museum traces the development of the city's port over the last 250 years. Special exhibitions highlight the Alexandria canal system. *Hours:* Tues-Fri, 11:00am-4:00pm; Sat-Sun, 1:00pm-4:00pm. *Address:* 44 Canal Center Plaza (703-838-4288).

Black History Resource Center

Alexandria's Black History Center offers exhibits and programs relating to black history and culture in Virginia and DC. *Hours:* Tues-Sat, 10:00am-4:00pm. *Address:* 638 N. Alfred St. (703-836-4356). **M**

Alexandria Gazette

Tours of the *Gazette*, one of the oldest daily newspapers in America, include the newsroom, composing room, and press plant. *Hours:* Mon-Fri, by appointment. *Address:* 717 N. Asaph St. (703-549-0004).

Green Spring Farm

Built sometime around 1760, the plantation house at Green Spring Farm today serves as headquarters for the Fairfax County Council of the Arts. The 17-acre estate and home host a variety of art shows and horticultural events throughout the year. *Hours:* daily (changing hours). *Address:* Green Spring Rd., off Route 236 (703-941-6066).

Fairfax County, VA

Collingwood Museum
The Collingwood Library and Museum is housed in the former home of George Washington's farm overseer. There's an extensive American heritage library with a special genealogical collection, as well as an eclectic selection of historical artifacts, such as the original Bowie knife and a set of Presidential china. *Hours:* Wed-Sun, 10:00am-4:00pm. *Address:* 8301 E. Boulevard Dr. (at Collingwood Rd. intersection) (703-765-1652). **T**

River Farm
Now headquarters of the American Horticultural Society, River Farm is a 25-acre estate once owned by George Washington. The gorgeous grounds are planted with wildflowers, orchards, and gardens; the walnut trees were planted by Washington himself. *Hours:* Mon-Fri, 10:00am-4:00pm. *Address:* E. Boulevard Dr. (Arcturus exit from G.W. Parkway) (703-768-5700).

Washington's Grist Mill
George Washington built this mill, now beautifully restored, to produce flour and corn meal for his kitchens and for export to England and the West Indies. Interpretive displays illustrate the workings of the 18th-century machinery. *Hours:* June-Aug: daily, 10:00am-5:00pm; Sept-May: Sat-Sun, 10:00am-5:00pm. *Address:* Mount Vernon Memorial Highway (703-339-7265). **C T**

Pohick Church

George Washington and Revolutionary War leader George Mason sat on the building committee for this dignified country parish church. Built between 1770 and 1774, it was badly damaged during the Civil War and used as a military stable for a time. Today, Pohick Church has been artfully restored to its original Colonial design. *Hours:* daily, 9:00am-4:00pm. *Address:* Richmond Highway at Telegraph Rd. (703-550-9449).

Army Engineer Museum

Located on the grounds of the old Belvoir estate near Mount Vernon, this interesting museum depicts the history and heroic deeds of the U.S. Army Corps of Engineers. Fort Belvoir also includes the archaeological dig at the original Belvoir Mansion, circa 1740. *Hours:* Wed-Sun, 9:00am-4:30pm. *Address:* 16th St. & Belvoir Rd. (703-664-6104). **C T**

Wildlife Preserve

The overlapping Mason Neck State Park and U.S. National Wildlife Preserve provide nearly 3,000 acres of protected habitat for deer, fox, muskrats, and 200 other species that live near Belmont Bay. The primary goal of the preserve is to encourage breeding of bald eagles. *Hours:* daily, 8:00am-sunset. *Address:* Gunston Road (Route 242) (703-339-7265). **C T**

Saint Mary's Church

Saint Mary's was constructed in 1858 for Irish immigrants who built the Orange and Alexandria Railroad. After the Civil War battles of Manassas and Chantilly, casualties were nursed at the church by Clara Barton, founder of the American Red Cross. *Hours:* daily, 9:00am-3:00pm. *Address:* Ox Road (Route 123) (703-978-4141). **T**

Colvin Run Mill

Colvin Run Mill has been grinding meal and flour with wooden gears and machinery since 1801. Nearby, the old Miller's House, built in 1818, has been transformed into a museum, and a 19th-century general store sells flour from the mill, local crafts, and food specialities. *Hours:* March-Dec: Wed-Mon, 10:00am-5:00pm. *Address:* 10017 Colvin Run Rd. at Route 7 (703-759-2771). **C**

Great Falls Park
The Potomac River makes a 76-foot plunge into the deep Mathers Gorge in Great Falls Park. This heavily wooded, 800-acre park provides a conducive environment for wildlife, and beaver, white-tailed deer, fox, possum, and raccoon abound. The park also includes two original locks built by George Washington's Patowmack Canal Company to circumvent the falls. *Hours:* daily, 8:00am-sunset. *Address:* Old Dominion Dr. (Route 738) (703-759-2915). **C T**

Wolf Trap Farm Park
Situated in 100 acres of rolling, wooded countryside, Wolf Trap Farm is the first national park for the performing arts. Admission to the park is free, and many performances, particularly those for children, are also without charge. *Hours:* daily (call for performance times). *Address:* 1624 Trap Rd., Vienna (703-255-1900 or 255-1898). **H C**

Freeman Store
Built in 1859 by a merchant from New Jersey, the Freeman Store has been a general store, military command post, hospital, train station, firehouse, and post office. Restored in 1975, the store now is a local museum and outlet for homemade crafts. *Hours:* Sat-Sun, 1:00pm-5:00pm. *Address:* 131 Church St., Vienna (703-938-5187).

Fairfax County Courthouse
Completed in 1800 and still in use as a judicial center, this Federal-style courthouse was restored in 1967. Many original Colonial documents kept there were lost during the Civil War, when Mosby's Rangers battled Union troops who had occupied the courthouse. However, the wills of George and Martha Washington were saved and are on display in the Clerk's office. *Hours:* Mon-Fri, 9:00am-4:30pm. *Address:* 4000 Chain Bridge Rd. at Main St., Fairfax (703-246-2421).

Prince William County, VA

Marine Corps Museum

Housed at the Quantico Marine Base, the Marine Corps Air and Ground Museum showcases Corps history with weapons, uniforms, military vehicles, and combat aircraft in restored hangars. The aircraft collection includes a Curtiss Pusher, a De Havilland bomber, a Japanese Zero, a Navy Hellcat, and a Boeing FB-5. *Hours:* April-Nov: Tues-Sun, 10:00am-5:00pm. *Address:* Route 619 (703-640-2606). **C T**

Manassas Museum

The Manassas City Museum, housed in a turn-of-the-century Victorian Romanesque bank, displays a variety of artifacts, including relics of the area's prehistoric inhabitants, Civil War items, 19th-century toys, and railroad memorabilia. *Hours:* Tues-Sun, 10:00am-5:00pm. *Address:* 9406 Main St. (703-368-1873). **C**

Occoquan Walking Tour

Occoquan, which comes from a Dogue Indian word meaning "end of the water," was first settled by Europeans in 1730. Today, the entire town is listed on the National Register of Historic Places. Pick-up a self-guided walking tour brochure at the Tourist Information Center on Mill Street. *Hours:* daily, 9:00am-5:00pm. (Phone: 703-491-4045). **H C T**

Manassas National Battlefield Park

Manassas National Battlefield Park

This national park preserves the tragic ground where the First and Second Battles of Manassas (Bull Run) were fought. On the stifling hot morning of July 21, 1861, Confederate troops rallied from what seemed sure defeat to rout raw Union volunteers. About a year later, Federal troops under General John Pope were again crushed at Bull Run Creek, paving the way for Lee's invasion of the North. An audio-visual show at the Visitors Center explains the battles. Guided walking tours are also offered three times daily during the summer. *Hours:* daily, 8:30am-5:00pm. *Address:* Route 234 (703-754-7107). **H C T**

Mill House Museum

Home to Occoquan millers from 1759 until 1925, the Merchant's Mill is now a local museum with relics and mementos of old Occoquan. *Hours:* daily, 11:00am-4:00pm. *Address:* 413 Mill St. (703-491-7525).

Weems-Botts Museum

Mason Locke Weems, better known as Parson Weems, biographer and contemporary of George Washington, owned this 18th-century building. His fanciful biography of Washington is responsible for perpetuating the story of the cherry tree and other questionable legends. The museum of local history is housed in Weems's bookstore. *Hours:* Mon-Sat, 10:00am-4:00pm; Sun, 1:00pm-4:00pm. *Address:* 300 Duke St., Dumfries (703-221-3346).

Montgomery County, MD

Glen Echo Cultural Arts Park

This unique attraction began in 1891 as the National Chautaqua Assembly, a center where DC residents could learn about the arts, science, literature, and languages. In 1899, the Assembly became a full-fledged amusement park with rides, carousels, and a ballroom. Now it has come full circle: under National Park Service management, Glen Echo is again a cultural arts center. Utilizing restored amusement park buildings, the center presents concerts, puppet shows, crafts demonstrations, dances, art shows, festivals, readings, and plays. *Hours:* Mon-Fri, 10:00am-5:00pm; Sat-Sun, noon-5:00pm. *Address:* McArthur Blvd. & Goldsboro Rd. (301-492-6282). **H C**

National Institutes of Health

The world-renowned NIH complex covers a 300-acre campus and is comprised of 13 research institutes. The Visitors Information Center in Building 10 features model labs, an audio-visual show, exhibits, and a lecture hall. Free tours are provided for members of the health professions and related fields. *Hours:* Mon-Fri, 9:00am-4:00pm. *Address:* Cedar Lane between Wisconsin Ave. & Route 187, Bethesda (301-496-1776). **M H T**

Cabin John Regional Park
Designed with children in mind, this park includes the Noah's Ark Petting Zoo, a miniature train ride, the Locust Grove Nature Center, an ice rink, hiking trails, picnic areas, and campsites. *Hours:* daily, 10:00am-sunset. *Address:* 7777 Democracy Blvd., Bethesda (301-299-4555 or 365-2530). **M C**

Woodend Mansion
Designed by John Russell Pope in 1928, Woodend is a Georgian Revival manor listed on the National Register of Historic Places. Situated in a 40-acre wildlife sanctuary, it now houses the Audubon Naturalist Society, one of DC's oldest environmental organizations. There are lovely trails through the gardens, greenhouses, and woods. *Hours:* Mon-Fri, 9:00am-5:00pm. *Address:* 8940 Jones Mill Rd., Chevy Chase (301-652-9188). **M**

McCrillis Gardens and Gallery
A branch of the Maryland-National Capital Park system, McCrillis Gardens cover five acres with 1,000 varieties of azaleas, rhododendrons, hollies, and exotic plants. The Gallery features prints, watercolors, and drawings from the Montgomery County Contemporary Art Collection. *Garden Hours:* daily, 10:00am-sunset. *Gallery Hours:* Sat-Sun, noon-4:00pm. *Address:* 6910 Greentree Rd., Bethesda (301-469-8438).

National Capital Trolley Museum
Built to resemble a 19th-century railway station, the Trolley Museum operates historic American and European trams and streetcars along its own tracks. In addition, there are films, exhibits depicting the history of trolleys, and model tram systems. *Hours:* Sat, Sun, & holidays, noon-5:00pm. *Address:* Bonifant Rd., N. Wheaton (301-384-6088). **C**

Washington Mormon Temple
The stunning, Oz-like Washington Temple of the Church of the Latter Day Saints is closed to non-Mormons, but the fascinating Visitors Center offers multi-media presentations, movies, and tours of the award-winning gardens. *Hours:* daily, 10:00am-9:30pm. *Address:* 9900 Stoneybrook Dr., Kensington (301-587-0144). **H C T**

Clara Barton House (Photo: National Park Service)

Clara Barton National Historic Site

Built in 1891, this curious Victorian house was originally a warehouse for Red Cross supplies. In 1897, Clara Barton moved into the modified building and made it her home and the American Red Cross headquarters. Most of the furnishings are original and include gifts of gratitude from foreign leaders for Barton's relief work during wars and natural disasters. *Hours:* daily, 10:00am-5:00pm. *Address:* 5801 Oxford Rd., Glen Echo (301-492-6245). **T**

Seventh Day Adventist World Headquarters

Stop by the Visitor Center for a tour of this fascinating religious and educational center. *Hours:* Mon-Fri, 9:00am-5:00pm. *Address:* 6930 Carrol Ave., Takoma Park (301-722-6000). **M T**

Strathmore Hall

This turn-of-the-century mansion is now the Montgomery County Arts Center, a charming venue for visual, performing, and literary arts events, which are held year-round. *Hours:* Mon-Fri, 10:00am-4:00pm; Sat, 10:00am-3:00pm. *Address:* 10701 Rockville Pike (301-530-0540). **M**

Brookside Gardens

There are always plants in bloom at the spectacular Brookside Gardens. The conservatories showcase colorful seasonal displays, lush tropical gardens, and bubbling brooks. Outside, there are formal gardens, as well as a Japanese Garden complete with authentic teahouse. *Grounds Hours:* daily, 9:00am-sunset. *Conservatories Hours:* daily, 9:00am-5:00pm. *Address:* 1500 Glenallan Ave., Wheaton (301-949-8230).

Wheaton Regional Park

This family-oriented, 500-acre park features a petting zoo, scenic train ride, a carousel, horseback riding, camping, ice skating, and picnic areas. *Hours:* daily, 9:00am-5:00pm. *Address:* Glenallan Ave., Wheaton (301-622-0056). **C**

National Geographic Society Center

The National Geographic Society Membership Center presents changing exhibits on archaeology, mapping, world cultures, and society-sponsored expeditions at this book and map outlet. *Hours:* Mon-Fri, 9:00am-4:00pm. *Address:* Darnestown Rd., Gaithersburg (301-921-1200).

Chesapeake & Ohio Canal Park

Wildlife and rugged beauty abound at this historic National Park along the Potomac River. This section of the Park includes the Great Falls and rapids, the Canal Museum, canal barge rides, original canal locks, and scenic nature trails. *Hours:* daily, 9:00am-5:00pm. *Address:* 11710 MacArthur Blvd., Potomac (301-299-3613 or 299-2026). **C**

Goldman Fine Arts Gallery

This unusual gallery exhibits contemporary and historical works of art dedicated to the Jewish cultural experience through the ages. *Hours:* Mon-Thurs, noon-9:00pm; Sun, 2:00pm-5:00pm. *Address:* 6125 Montrose Rd., Rockville (301-881-0100). **M**

Prince Georges County, MD

Agricultural Research Center

The U.S. Department of Agriculture's Research Center incorporates over 7,000 acres of experimental farms, orchards, pastures, barns, gardens, labs, and greenhouses. Since 1910, ARC scientists have been solving problems in agriculture, nutrition, and ecology. The two-hour guided tour (by appointment) is informative and interesting. Self-guided tours are also possible. *Hours:* Mon-Fri, 8:00am-4:30pm. *Address:* Beaver Dam Rd., off Edmonston Rd., Beltsville (301-344-2483 or 344-2403). **C T**

Air & Space Reserve Collection

The Paul E. Garber Preservation and Storage Facility houses the National Air & Space Museum's reserve collection of historic airplanes and spacecraft. This "no frills" museum displays almost 100 aircraft, along with spacecraft, satellites, and other flight-related items. The behind-the-scenes tour includes a rare opportunity to observe the restoration and preservation process. *Hours:* Mon-Fri, 10:00am-noon; Sat-Sun, 10:00am & 1:00pm. *Address:* Old Silver Hill Rd., Suitland (202-357-1400). **C T**

College Park Airport Museum

The world's oldest continuously operating airfield, the College Park Airport is second only in importance to Kitty Hawk in the

The NASA/Goddard Space Flight Center

early development of American aviation. In 1910, the Wright Brothers trained the U.S. Army's first pilots to fly there. Displays explore the many aviation firsts that took place at College Park between 1909 and 1939. *Hours:* Mon-Fri, noon-4:00pm. *Address:* Corporal Frank Scott Dr., College Park (301-779-2011).

NASA/Goddard Space Flight Center

NASA's Visitor Center and Museum provides an exciting over-view of the history and heroics of space flight. Tours of specialized working areas, such as NASA tracking operations, can be arranged. There are walking tours each Thursday and rock-et launches on Sundays at 1:00pm. *Hours:* Wed-Sun, 10:00am-4:00pm. *Address:* Soil Conservation Rd., Greenbelt (301-286-8981). **C T**

Andrews Air Force Base

Established in 1942 by Presidential Order, this 4,200-acre base is headquarters for the Strategic Air Command, Continental Air Command, and the Military Airlift Command, as well as home to Air Force, Navy, and Marine units. Andrews is best known as the home of Air Force One and the Presidential air fleet. There are 90-minute tours on Mondays and Fridays during the summer and by reservation throughout the year. *Address:* Exit 9 off I-495, Camp Springs (301-981-4511). **C T**

Civil War re-enactment at Fort Washington
(Photo: National Park Service)

Oxon Hill Farm
Kids love to visit Oxon Hill, an authentic turn-of-the-century working farm run by the National Park Service. Daily farm activities, such as milking, cider-pressing, sheep-shearing, planting, threshing, molasses-making, and harvesting are still done the old-fashioned way at Oxon Hill. *Hours:* daily, 8:30am-5:00pm. *Address:* 6411 Oxon Hill Rd., Oxon Hill (301-839-1177). **C T**

Equestrian Center
Prince Georges County Equestrian Center features riding events and horse shows year-round. Dressage, thoroughbred training trials, barrel-racing championships, and appaloosa and quarter horse shows are just a sample of the free events. *Hours:* Call for show times. *Address:* 14955 Pennsylvania Ave., Upper Marlboro (301-627-6727 or 952-4740).

Watkins Regional Park
Watkins Park has a historic carousel, the Old Maryland Farm, a miniature train ride, campgrounds, and picnic areas. *Park Hours:* daily, 7:30am-dusk. *Farm Hours:* Mon-Fri, 9:30am-2:30pm; Sat-Sun, 11:00am-4:00pm. *Address:* Watkins Park Dr., Upper Marlboro (301-249-7077 or 249-6900). **C**

Fort Washington
Little altered since its completion in 1824, Fort Washington is a splendid example of an early 19th-century coastal defense. Designed to withstand attack by naval vessels, its high masonry walls, drawbridge, and dry moat illustrate many principles of early military science and architecture. Today, the fort displays artillery, ramparts, barracks, and officer's quarters and has interpretive history tours and events. *Hours:* May-Aug: daily, 7:30am-8:00pm; Sept-April: daily, 7:30am-5:00pm. *Address:* Fort Washington Rd. off Route 210, Silesia (301-763-4600). **C T**

Patuxent River Park
Covering almost 6,000 acres, the Patuxent River Park includes the Jug Bay Natural Area, the Black Walnut Creek Nature Study Area, Patuxent Cultural Village, nature trails, and wildlife conservation areas. Guided tours and demonstrations at the Living History Area, with its early 19th-century village, provide a

glimpse of what life was like on the river 150 years ago. *Hours:* daily, 8:00am-dusk. *Address:* Croom Airport Rd., Upper Marlboro (301-627-6074). **C T**

University of Maryland Art Gallery

The University Art Gallery presents changing exhibitions year-round, as well as objects from its permanent collections of African, American, and European art. *Hours:* Mon-Fri, 10:00am-4:00pm; Sat-Sun, 1:00pm-5:00pm. *Address:* 2200 Arts Building, College Park (301-454-2763).

Montpelier Mansion

Built by Major Thomas Snowden in 1770, Montpelier Mansion is now the site of Prince Georges Cultural Arts Center, where artists and craftspeople hold exhibitions and demonstrations daily. *Hours:* daily, 10:00am-5:00pm. *Address:* 12826 Laurel Bowie Rd., Laurel (301-779-2011 or 953-1993).

Belair Mansion and Stable Museum

Belair Mansion was built around 1740 for Maryland's Governor Samuel Ogle. From 1899 to 1955, it was owned by the Woodwards, a prominent horse racing family. Today, both the Mansion and the stables are museums. *Hours:* Sun, 1:00pm-4:00pm. *Address:* 12207 Tulip Grove Dr., Bowie (301-262-6200).

Annual Events

January

1st Week: Congress convenes.

3rd Monday: Martin Luther King Jr. Birthday Observance, marked by speeches and performances around DC, plus a wreath-laying ceremony at the Lincoln Memorial.

19th: Robert E. Lee Birthday Celebration in Arlington National Cemetery, featuring 19th-century music and food.

Late Jan.: Chinese New Year parade and festival on H St., between 5th and 8th Sts.

February

Entire Month: Black History Month celebrated with special museum exhibits, performances, and shows.

12th: Abraham Lincoln's Birthday commemorated by services at the Lincoln Memorial and programs at Ford's Theatre.

14th: Frederick Douglass' Birthday marked at Cedar Hill.

20th: Revolutionary War Encampment at Fort Ward Park (4301 W. Braddock Rd., Alexandria, VA) features skirmishes and period costumes.

21st: George Washington's Birthday is celebrated at Mount Vernon with services and free tours. Old Town Alexandria puts on the nation's biggest parade, and DC marks the day with colorful ceremonies at the Washington Monument.

March

2nd Sunday: St. Patrick's Day Parade along Constitution Avenue at 1:00pm.

Last Saturday: Kite Festival on the Washington Monument grounds from 10am-4pm, sponsored by the Smithsonian.

April

1st Week: Cherry Blossom Festival, with concerts, a parade, and the ceremonial lighting of the Japanese Lantern at the Tidal Basin. Call 202-737-2599 for information.

4th: White House Easter Egg Roll for children 8 and under (accompanied by an adult) on the South Lawn. Enter through the southeast gate of the White House on East Executive Ave.

13th: Thomas Jefferson's Birthday is marked by wreath-laying ceremonies at his Memorial at 11am.

Mid-April: White House Spring Garden Tours.

22nd: Earth Day is celebrated with special events on the Mall.

4th Weekend: Alexandria's Pan-American Festival at Oronoco Bay Park celebrates Latin American culture.

23rd: William Shakespeare's birthday is celebrated at the Folger Shakespeare Library from 11am-4pm.

30th: Duke Ellington's birthday prompts a party at Freedom Plaza (13th and Pennsylvania Ave., NW) from noon-6pm.

May

1st Sunday: Bethesda-Chevy Chase Parade with music, entertainment, and rides at Bethesda Metro Plaza.

1st Weekend: Washington National Cathedral Flower Mart, saluting a different country each year with flower booths, decorating tips, and entertainment.

1st Weekend: Alexandria's Annual Arts & Crafts Fair at the Market Square.

13th: Annual National Law Enforcement Officers Memorial Candlelight Vigil honors fallen police officers and officially dedicates new names to the Memorial, located at E & F and 4th & 5th Streets, NW.

14th: Dept. of Defense Open House at Andrews Air Base.

21st: Alexandria's Polish Festival at the Market Square.

3rd Weekend: Greek Spring Festival at Sts. Constantine & Helen Greek Orthodox Church (4115 16th St., NW).

Memorial Day: Special services at the Vietnam Veterans Memorial and Arlington National Cemetery. Free Jazz Festival at Oronoco Bay Park, Alexandria. Free evening concert by National Symphony at Capitol's West Lawn.

Throughout the Summer

Tuesdays: Marine Corps Sunset Parades at the Iwo Jima Memorial in Arlington, VA begin at 7:00pm. Call 202-433-4173 for details.

The Navy Band gives free concerts at the U.S. Navy Memorial on Pennsylvania Ave. Tuesday evenings at 8pm.

Wednesdays: "Music Under the Stars," a free concert at the Sylvan Theatre on the grounds of the Washington Monument, features big band sounds from 7pm-9pm.

A multimedia show called "The American Sailor" showcasing the history of the Navy begins at 6:30pm at the Washington Navy Yard. Call 202-433-2218 for reservations.

The Twilight Tattoo Series, which runs mid-July to late August, combines music and marching on the Ellipse grounds between the White House and the Washington Monument. It starts at 7pm. For details, call 703-696-3570.

Fridays: Marine Corps Evening Parades start each Friday at 8:45pm at the Marine Barracks, 8th & I Sts., SE. To assure a seat, make reservations at 202-433-6060.

Saturdays: The Iwo Jima Memorial is also the site of carillon recitals from 6:30pm-8:30pm each Saturday.

Sundays: Watch free polo matches each Sunday afternoon on the field east of the Lincoln Memorial. Call 202-619-7222 for more details.

June

1st Weekend: Dupont-Kalorama Museum Walk.

1st Weekend: DC Potomac Riverfest with tall ships, fireworks, boat rides, and music.

4th: Philippine Independence Day parade and fair on Pennsylvania Ave. from 4th-13th Streets, NW.

11th: Marvin Gaye Appreciation Day honors the DC-born entertainer. 13th-14th Streets & Pennsylvania Ave., NW.

2nd Weekend: Alexandria Waterfront Festival features tall ships, arts and crafts, music, and fireworks.

4th Weekend: Alexandria's "Fair in the Square" celebrates Jewish-American Culture at Chinquapin Park.

July

First Week: Smithsonian Annual Festival of American Folklore highlights different cultures on the National Mall.

4th: Independence Day celebrations include parades, fife and drum performances, military band concerts, and an evening performance by the National Symphony Orchestra at the Capitol's West Lawn. The festivities culminate in a spectacular fireworks display over the Washington Monument.

8th: Alexandria's Birthday marked by live entertainment and fireworks at Jones Point Park.

1st Weekend: The D.C. Free Jazz Festival lures jazz lovers to the concerts at Freedom Plaza, 1300 Pennsylvania Ave., NW.

14th: The hilarious Bastille Day Waiters' Race festivities begins at noon at 20th and Pennsylvania Ave., NW.

Mid-July: Caribbean Summer in the Park celebrates island culture at Lot #8, RFK Stadium.

3rd Saturday: Alexandria Italian Festival at the Market Square.

Last Weekend: DC Hispanic Festival in Adams-Morgan with music, dance, food, arts, and crafts.

August

1st Saturday: Alexandria Irish Festival at the Market Square.

Mid-August: The Thai Heritage Festival honors Thailand at the Smithsonian's Museum of Natural History.

15th: The Army Band performs the *1812 Overture* at the Sylvan Theatre.

Mid-August: The Children's Lollipop Concert by the Navy Band is a special program geared to kids at the Sylvan Theatre on the Washington Monument grounds at 8pm.

3rd Saturday: Capital Classic Horse Show at Prince Georges County Equestrian Center.

3rd Saturday: Alexandria Scottish Festival celebrates the city's early settlers at the Market Square.

Last Weekend: Georgia Avenue Day celebrates DC's longest business corridor. Georgia Ave. at Eastern Ave., NW.

September

1st Weekend: The National Frisbee Festival spins out of control on the Mall near the Air & Space Museum.

1st Weekend: The DC Blues Festival features top performers in Anacostia Park.

Labor Day: The National Symphony Orchestra presents a free concert on the Capitol's West Lawn at 2:00pm.

2nd Weekend: The Black Family Reunion celebrates the African-American family on the Mall.

2nd Sunday: Adams-Morgan day is celebrated with international music, food, dance, and crafts.

17th: On the anniversary of the signing of the U.S. Constitution, the entire document is displayed at the National Archives, and there's a variety of ceremonies.

4th Saturday: Alexandria Afro-American Festival at the Market Square.

4th Weekend: Rock Creek Park celebrates with environmental exhibits, international music, arts and crafts, and recreational activities for children.

October

1st Saturday: Washington Cathedral Open House features tours and demonstrations of stained glass, stone and wood carving, and organ recitals.

10th: Various groups honor Christopher Columbus at the Columbus Memorial Plaza in front of Union Station.

11th: The U.S. Navy Band celebrates the birthday of the Navy with a concert in the Kennedy Center. Free, but pick up tickets early to assure seating.

Mid-Oct: White House Fall Garden Tour.

28th: Alexandria Annual Antique Show at Market Square.

4th Saturday: Georgetown Halloween Parade.

November

1st Weekend: The Navy Museum celebrates maritime lore with its annual Seafaring Celebration in Bldg. 76 at the Washington Navy Yard.

11th: Veteran's Day ceremonies at Arlington National Cemetery.

December

1st Saturday: Alexandria Christmas Scottish Walk with a parade of bagpipers, Scottish clans, and special children's events in the Old Town.

1st Weekend: The U.S. Army Band gives a holiday concert at D.A.R. Constitution Hall. Free, but you need tickets to assure seating. Call 703-696-3399 for details.

3rd Weekend: The Navy Band plays holiday favorites at the same location. Call ahead for ticket details (202-433-2525).

15th: White House Christmas Tree-lighting at the Ellipse.

Mid-Dec.: Poinsettia lovers should head for the U.S. Botanic Gardens for its Christmas Poinsettia Show, featuring over 3,500 holiday plants.

24th & 25th: Washington National Cathedral offers special services and choral performances for Christmas. Call 202-537-6200 for details.

28th-30th: From 5pm-7pm, the White House gives free tours of its Christmas decorations. The tours are very popular, so show up early.

31st: New Year's Eve revelry at the Old Post Office Pavilion.

More Great Travel Books
from Mustang Publishing

Europe for Free by Brian Butler. If you're on a tight budget—or if you just love a bargain—this is the book for you! With descriptions of thousands of things to do and see for free all over Europe, you'll save lots of lira, francs, and pfennigs. *"Well-organized and packed with ideas"—Modern Maturity.* **$9.95**

Also in this series:

London for Free by Brian Butler. **$8.95**

Hawaii for Free by Frances Carter. **$8.95**

The Southwest for Free by Mary Jane & Greg Edwards. **$8.95**

Paris for Free (Or Extremely Cheap) by Mark Beffart. **$8.95**

Australia: Where the Fun Is by Goodyear & Skinner. From the best pubs in Sydney to the cheapest motels in Darwin to the greatest hikes in Tasmania, this guide by two recent Yale grads details all the fun stuff Down Under—on and off the beaten path. *"Indispensable"—Library Journal.* **$12.95**

Bet On It! The Ultimate Guide to Nevada by Mary Jane & Greg Edwards. What does it mean when there's a cup over the handle of a slot machine? When should you buy "insurance" in blackjack? Which hotels have the best deals in Las Vegas? Is there good fishing near Reno? **Bet On It!** can answer all those questions and more. It's a complete handbook on all the casino games, plus an up-to-date guide to Nevada's best—and best-avoided—hotels, attractions, and tourist activities. A sure bet for anyone going to Nevada! *"Amusing and useful"—New York Daily News.* **$10.95**

France on the TGV: How to Use the World's Fastest Train to Get the Most out of France by Mark Beffart. Imagine boarding a train in Paris in the morning and arriving in Nice—almost 700 miles away—in time to get a suntan! With the TGV, the world's fastest train, it's easy, and this book describes everything you need to know to use this *magnifique* rail network. From descriptions of the myriad rail passes available to walking tours of over 50 French towns served by the TGV, it's a must for today's high-speed traveler. *"An exceptionally useful guide"—Atlanta Constitution.* **$12.95**

Let's Blow thru Europe by Thomas Neenan & Greg Hancock. The essential guide for the "15-cities-in-14-days" traveler, this is the funniest, most irreverent, and definitely most honest travel guide ever written. With this book, you can blow off the boring museums and minor cathedrals and instead find the great bars, restaurants, and fun stuff in all the major cities of Europe. *"A riot!"—The Daily Northwestern (Northwestern U.).* **$10.95**

Mustang books should be available at your local bookstore. If not, send a check or money order for the price of the book, plus $1.50 postage *per book*, to Mustang Publishing, P.O. Box 3004, Memphis, TN 38173 U.S.A. Allow three weeks for delivery. For rush, one-week delivery, add $3.00 to the total. *International orders:* Please pay in U.S. funds, and add $5.00 to the total for Air Mail.

For a complete catalog of Mustang books, send $1.00 and a stamped, self-addressed, business-size envelope to Catalog Request, Mustang Publishing, P.O. Box 3004, Memphis, TN 38173.